When Dr. Eric Chaffin identifies 'an exceptional sensitivity to the voice of God' as one of the evidences of a powerful prayer life, he goes to the heart of what God wants to accomplish in our lives. So how does a Christian develop a powerful prayer life? Open up *Faint Not: Powerful Prayer Along the Broken Road* and let Eric point you in the right direction.

—Dennis D. Frey, Th.D.,
president, Master's International School of Divinity

Eric Chaffin has done it! In *Faint Not: Powerful Prayer Along the Broken Road*, he has accomplished the difficult task of taking prayer from mechanical and dutiful to personal and powerful—not an easy task. I strongly recommend this work as a must read for the growing believer.

—Dr. Johnie Butler, pastor,
The Lighthouse Church, Pembroke Pines, FL

Eric has provided a wonderful resource in Faint *Not: Powerful Prayer Along the Broken Road*, which takes a strong biblical approach to prayer. Many writers have jumped straight in to the topic without considering the nature of prayer. Eric begins with a fundamental understanding and then proceeds to walk the reader through very keen insights on prayer from God's Word. His personal observations and transparency on the journey are refreshing.

—Kenneth Priest, director of Convention Strategies, Southern Baptists of Texas

Faint Not

Faint Not: Powerful Prayer Along The Broken Road

~ Eric Chaffin

TATE PUBLISHING
AND ENTERPRISES, LLC

Published by Tate Publishing & Enterprises, LLC
127 E. Trade Center Terrace | Mustang, Oklahoma 73064 USA
1.888.361.9473 | www.tatepublishing.com

Tate Publishing is committed to excellence in the publishing industry. The company reflects the philosophy established by the founders, based on Psalm 68:11,
"The Lord gave the word and great was the company of those who published it."

Cover design by Greg McCool and Samson Lim
Interior design by Jomar Ouano

Published in the United States of America

ISBN: 978-1-68142-572-6
Religion / Christian Life / Prayer
15.06.17

For the people of Southcrest

Contents

Contents

Introduction

There was an ironic sentiment found in a love song popularized by the country group Rascal Flatts, "This much I know is true, that God blessed the broken road that led me straight to you."[1]

I find that there is actually a nugget of theological truth in that statement; a truth not only borne by the scriptures, but one I have even seen on display in my own life.

That truth is: God often allows a broken road to come into our lives, a wilderness experience of trial and testing. And while He is not always the cause of our wilderness sojourn, in his infinite wisdom, power and sovereignty, He is able to use those circumstances to lead us to a place He desires us to be—all the while molding us, guiding us, teaching us, breaking our will and transforming us in the process.

---

1 Bobby Boyd, Jeffrey Hanna and Marcus Hummon, *Bless The Broken Road* (Los Angeles: Bug Music, 1994)

For us, this wilderness can take on any number of forms—a broken marriage, a bankruptcy, acute loneliness, the death of a loved one, even the unfortunate consequences we suffer due to our own rebellion against God.

For some people, their response to the wilderness experience can often dictate whether this sojourn of trials is one of peace or turmoil, one of reward or regret, whether the path traversed is circuitous or straight, and whether the journey is lengthy or brief.

This wilderness experience is epitomized by God's people, the Israelites. After Joseph died, the Israelites living in Egypt fell out of favor with their Egyptian rulers and were forced into slavery. God sent Moses who, having the benefit of ten plagues from God that forced the Egyptian pharaoh to release them, was able to lead the Israelites out of Egyptian bondage toward a land promised to them by God. This journey was by way of the Sinai desert, however; and it was in the Sinai that God's people learned how and how not to respond to diversity.

As we read the Israelites' story, we see a pattern of response to their wilderness circumstances begin to form. Rather than choosing to reflect on the supernatural displays of might that God exhibited on their behalf in order to lead and protect them, or to see that their trials were producing godly character in them such as patience, submission, and perseverance, or to recognize their situation for what it was—an opportunity to see God's trustworthiness firsthand—what did they do?

They grumbled. They murmured. They complained. They bellyached. It began not too long after God delivered the Israelites from the pursuit of the Egyptian army with a miraculous parting of the Red Sea.

It started with complaints like,

- What are we going to drink? (Exod. 15:24, 17:3).
- Are you going to let us die of hunger out here? (Exod. 16:3).
- Oh, manna again? We are tired of manna! We want meat! (Num. 11:4–6).
- They expressed dissatisfaction with Moses' leadership (Exod. 32:23, Num. 12:1).

So great was the Israelite's complaining, that it became habitual and destructive. The people even accused God of leading them into the wilderness just to die (Exod. 17:3). Ultimately, because they chose not to trust God, the Israelites took forty years to make a trip that should have only required an eleven-day walk!

Like the Israelites, our human existence is full of all sorts of obstacles, trials, and *curveballs* the circumstances of life throw at us. More often than not, we have absolutely no control whatsoever over these situations. We can, however, choose how we will respond to the hurt, to the suffering, to the awful things that people say and do to us. Even not choosing how to respond is a response in itself. For better or for worse, we will always make a choice.

The unfortunate reality is that many people choose self-destructive responses rather than healthy, godly ones. When a negative circumstance occurs, some may choose to cope with it using any number of things—with food, with chemical substances, by shutting others out of their lives, by giving up hope, by constant grumbling—all things that, given the situation, can be harmful to physical, emotional, and spiritual health. Some of us might give in to uncontrolled rage or plot to vengefully do harm to those we deem responsible for our situation. Rather than turning to chemical substances, others may self-medicate using a retail *drug*, maxing out credit cards with out-of-control spending.

These responses are unfortunate enough, but a bigger problem occurs in that human beings are creatures of habit. The more we turn to unhealthy coping mechanisms, the more we become ingrained in self-destructive and, often, ungodly behavior. Nouthetic (Bible-based) counselors call this the doctrine of habituation.

A behavioral pattern develops: Jeff's boss berates him at work. Jeff deals with it by getting drunk that night. The verbal abuse continues over the course of weeks, months. Each time, Jeff chooses to cope with alcohol.

Without realizing it, Jeff's pattern of response has introduced him to a new problem—alcoholism.

But let's ponder a hypothetical *what if* for a moment.

What would happen if we chose to respond to every negative stimulus—the hurtful word, the bank overdraft, the company pink slip, the sudden illness, the interstate blowout, the betrayal of a close friend or spouse—with prayer?

What if instead of resorting to the habitual coping mechanisms we resort to in the midst of our broken road experiences, we passionately sought out the heart and will of God?

What if we embarked on a new course of discipline, retraining ourselves to respond to each of life's new roadblocks by saying something like this?

> Father, I cannot understand what is happening in my life right now. I'm hurting, and I am confused. But, Lord, I know that you are in still in control and that you will always love me. I realize that my circumstance did not take you by surprise, and I'm also fully aware that you can take any amount of trial or suffering I encounter and use it to accomplish whatever purposes you deem necessary in my life. I have many questions, and while I can't see what the immediate future holds, I know that you are the architect of my future. Even though I do not feel your presence at this moment, I believe you are with me, Lord. I praise you that you are trustworthy. Today I choose to trust you.

Oh, if only we could respond to the broken road with immediate and continual praise and prayers of our expressed trust in God. And how unfortunate it is that Christians do not seek God as fervently when they are on the mountaintop as they do when they are in the desert!

Matthew Henry once wrote, "When troubles last long, even good men are tempted to entertain hard thoughts of God. Therefore He will not contend forever, for He will not forsake the work of His own hands."[2]

We might second-guess Him while we're traversing the broken road, but God is on our side, and though we might think it, He will not abandon us. He is at work even when we cannot see it, and eventually, we learn that life's broken roads are a crucible—one in which we discover that prayer is our only recourse in dealing with hard circumstances. It is often from within our wilderness experiences that the great power of prayer and praise is experienced.

Pastor Rick Warren, author of the best-selling *Purpose-Driven Life* once stated, "The deepest level of worship is praising God in spite of pain, thanking God during a trial, trusting Him when tempted, surrendering while suffering, and loving Him when He seems distant."[3]

---

2 Matthew Henry, *Matthew Henry's Concise Commentary On The Whole Bible* (Nashville: Thomas Nelson, Inc., 1977), 687.

3 Rick Warren, *The Purpose-Driven Life: What on Earth am I Here For?* (Grand Rapids: Zondervan Publishing, 2002), Kindle e-book.

To successfully navigate the broken road, however, that long wilderness sojourn must become a journey of persistent prayer. That word *persist* means *to continue firmly in a course of action despite difficulty, opposition or failure.* A Christ follower must learn to not only persist, but to do so trusting fully that God will turn ashes into gold—a gold of God's choosing, His making, and one granted in His timing. God can make the broken road something beautiful.

In the pages ahead, it is my intention to ask some basic questions like, "What is prayer?" and "Why should I pray?" Then together, we will explore some of the model prayers shown to us through the scriptures.

We will also delve into some deeper questions like, "Why do I pray God's will instead of my own?" and "What if God says no?"

We will study the biblical case for persistent prayer and conclude our journey of prayer together by exploring the abundant riches of continual, fervent prayer—the silver linings in dark clouds, the lessons learned along the broken road, the joy in the journey, and much more.

Whether you, like King David, are thirsting for God amid a dry and parched land (Psalm 63:1) or just see a need that should consistently be brought before the Lord, it is both my sincere prayer and my firm conviction that the pages ahead will work in your life to create a more intimate walk with God.

When you step on to the broken road (and believe me, at some point, you will), will you grumble and complain against God? Or will you acknowledge his trustworthiness, having discovered firsthand that, yes, there is power on the path of persistent prayer?

The Nature of Prayer

It is only fitting that we begin our exploration of powerful, persistent prayer with a simple question—what is prayer?

How do we define it? Is prayer talking to God? Asking God for help? Confession of our sins? Praising God for his wonderful attributes? A spiritual intervention on behalf of a loved one?

The truth is, it is all these things and much more. But before we delve into more detailed aspects of prayer, we must begin with a basic understanding of the concept.

It should be noted that in order to more efficiently facilitate our exploration of this topic, there are some peripheral questions connected to prayer that we will put aside.

Questions like,

- Is it best to pray standing up or sitting down?
- Kneeling or bowing down?
- Should our hands be open, closed, or lifted up to God?

- Eyes open or eyes closed?
- Should we pray in the morning or at night before bed? Do we pray privately or publicly?

These questions are not particularly relevant to our discussion since they do not involve prerequisites for prayer, but are primarily matters of personal preference.

What Prayer Is Not

In defining prayer, perhaps we can gain a clearer understanding by first establishing some things that prayer is not.

One thing that prayer definitely is not is a magic formula we use to talk God into something. Richard Chenevix Trench once said, "We must not conceive of prayer as overcoming God's reluctance, but as laying hold of His highest willingness."[1]

Dr. Adrian Rogers articulated the thought more simply:

> Prayer is not an exercise where we bend God's will and make it fit our will. Too many people have the notion that prayer is talking God into doing something that He ordinarily would not want to do.

---

1 Richard Chenevix Trench quoted in *The Kneeling Christian* (Grand Rapids: Zondervan Publishing House, 1945), 52.

> This is not true. Prayer is seeking the will of God and following it.[2]

Prayer is also not asking God for stuff. God is not a celestial genie or some sort of spiritual Santa Claus who grants our every whim. It does not matter how greatly we desire a red Corvette or a condo in the Caribbean. God's greatest priority is not our material greed. But He does stand ready to provide for the needs of his children who seek Him (Matt. 6:33).

Another thing prayer is not is a formal addressing of God employing flowery, King-James speech or verbalizing our thoughts like some would-be Shakespeare who bombastically prays in old English or poetic meter.

I cannot imagine my son coming home from school one day and saying, "I greet thee, most worthy father, and hail thee, eminent pastor and patriarch of our clan. Wouldst thou welcome me into thine home with thy blessing? And, gracious father, wouldst thou in thine infinite mercy grant to me, thine firstborn son, payment for yonder cafeteria lady, for mine lunch account droppeth into the red?"

No such formality is needed. Simple, conversational thoughts will do nicely.

Contrary to what many might believe, prayer is not recitation. We often hear some prayers beautifully recited,

---

2 Adrian Rogers, *What Every Christian Ought To Know* (Nashville: Broadman & Holman, 2005), 216.

particularly the Lord's Prayer found in Matthew 6 and Luke 11. It certainly sounds poignant when recited, even more so when sung.

But generally speaking, a prayer recited is not a prayer at all. It becomes something mechanically, habitually voiced by rote.

In Matthew 6:7, Jesus warns us about meaningless repetition—in this case, the nonsensical babbling of the same mantra over and over as the pagans did when they tried to pray to their false gods.

We must bear in mind that God is a spiritual being. When we speak to him, it must be from an outpouring of the heart, or more to the point, our spirit. Romans 8:16 says, "The Spirit himself testifies with our spirit that we are God's children." Whether we choose to verbalize our prayers or pray silently (just as AT&T serves as the phone service carrier that connects little Johnny with grandma), we actually communicate with God as our spirit connects with Him by way of his Holy Spirit, with Jesus serving as the operator.[3]

The question of whether recited prayer is genuine prayer rests upon the question of origin. From where do the words emanate? Is the prayer just an exercise in redundancy like the cutesy God-is-great, God-is-good prayers we routinely mutter over the evening meal? Or is it a plea to God from the innermost depth of our being?

---

3 More on this in Chapter 3, *The Paradigm of Prayer.*

It can also be stated unequivocally that prayer is not wishful desire or even positive thinking. While positive thoughts are a good thing, they will not produce the results that prayer does.

A boy once came to his dad and said, "Dad, I think I flunked my math test."

The dad said, "That's negative thinking. You've got to be more positive, son."

The boy replied, "I'm positive I flunked it!"

Likewise, prayer is not some vague hope or a general sense of nonspecific, undirected faith that believes everything will turn out fine.

True faith has an object—God.

And genuine prayer has a focus—God's will.

What Prayer Is

Now that we have established some things that prayer clearly is not, we should now begin to define what prayer actually is. Many have offered definitions of prayer (some more successfully than others), but let's examine the commonality we find in each of them.

One definition states that prayer is to converse with God; the intercourse of the soul with God, not in contemplation or meditation, but in direct address to him. Prayer may be oral or mental, occasional, or constant.[4]

According to the *Baker Evangelical Dictionary of Biblical Theology,* the general concept of prayer seen in both the Old and New Testaments is the simple belief that God could be petitioned to intervene and effect changes in nature and in the course of world events.[5]

Randy Hatchett describes prayer in a more specific way: "Dialogue between God and people, especially His covenant partners."[6]

Who are His covenant partners? Under the old covenant, that would be Israel. Under the new covenant established by Christ, that would be anyone who, by faith, has received Christ's gift of salvation and eternal life—in simpler terms, born-again Christians.

Dr. Greg Frizzell, a noted expert on spiritual renewal, defines prayer as "God's primary means of our coming to

---

4 *Prayer*, Easton's Bible Dictionary, Millenium3 Online Digital Library http://odl.mdivs.edu/dic/ebd/view.cgi?number=T2998 (accessed May 7, 2013)

5 *Prayer*, Baker's Evangelical Dictionary of Biblical Theology, Millenium3 Online Digital Library http://odl.mdivs.edu/dic/bed/view.cgi?number=T563 (accessed May 7, 2013)

6 Randy Hatchett, *Holman Illustrated Bible Dictionary* , ed. Trent C. Butler (Nashville: Holman Bible Publishers, 2003), 1320.

know Him, worship Him, and experience transformation through the indwelling Christ."[7]

Pastor Ronnie Floyd stated, "Prayer is a relationship, a fellowship that occurs between you and God. Prayer is the vehicle that takes you into the privilege of experiencing fellowship with God.[8]

While all of the above definitions have great merit and insight, sometimes the simplest is the best. I prefer the definition proposed by Dr. Tom Elliff who wrote, "Prayer is, above all else, communion with God."[9]

The simple truth is that God is our heavenly Father, and those of us adopted into His family by faith in Christ are His children. It naturally follows then that every child can and should talk to his or her Father.

What is vital—especially when traversing life's broken roads—is the time spent talking with God. This talk might be straightforward and simple, or it might be complex and multifaceted. Your conversation with God might bear the likeness of praise, petition, confession, intercession, thanksgiving, or any number of other forms. It might be talking to God while happy or sad. It could be talking

---

7 Gregory R. Frizzell, *How to Develop a Powerful Prayer Life* (Memphis: Master Design Ministries, 1999), 2.

8 Ronnie W. Floyd, *How to Pray: Developing an Intimate Relationship with God* (Nashville: Word Publishing/Thomas Nelson, Inc., 1999), Kindle e-book.

9 Tom Elliff, *A Passion for Prayer: Experiencing Deeper Intimacy with God* (Wheaton: Crossway Books/Good News Publishers, 1998), 34.

to God when feeling angry or confessing sin. It might be calling upon Him when feeling a sense of urgency or sensing a looming threat. Or it could even be crying out to God when departure from this life seems imminent.

Whatever the particular form, this is the essence of prayer: It is having a heart-to-heart conversation with God.

The Necessity of Prayer

Now that we have answered the question, "What is prayer?" we turn our attention to the next logical question as we search for purpose along the broken road.

Why should we pray?

Why is it necessary?

For every believer in Jesus Christ, this is a legitimate question (one that must be asked if we are to perform an adequate exploration of this subject).

Watchman Nee, a Chinese church leader and teacher, once pondered the same thought.

> Why pray? What is the use of praying? Is not God omniscient as well as omnipotent? Why must He wait till we pray before He commences to work? Since He knows, why must we tell Him everything?[1]

---

1 Watchman Nee, Let Us Pray translated from Chinese (Richmond: Christian Fellowship Publishers, 1977), 2.

To phrase it more concisely, why not just entrust our lives to the sovereignty of God without engaging in any sort of communication with Him?

In tackling that question, we hearken back to the famous quote from George Mallory who, when asked why he wanted to climb Mount Everest, replied, "Because it's there."

By the same token, the most obvious reason we Christians pray is because we can!

We would do well to remember the price that was paid to grant us a High Priest, Jesus Christ, that we might "approach God's throne of grace with confidence" (Heb. 4:14–16). The shed blood of Jesus on the cross of Calvary purchased that privilege. Why would we not want to take advantage of such a valuable opportunity obtained in such a costly way? Why would we not want to fellowship with the God whom we love because "He first loved us?" (1 John 4:19).

While our discussion of this question of *why*? is by no means exhaustive, it will illustrate seven of the most important reasons to seek the Lord in prayer.

God's Written Command for Us

One reason a Christian should pray is because it is something God commanded us to do. His Word is replete with instructions, not only for God's people to pray to him, but how to do so.

We are told to pray at all times. The Apostle Paul, in his first epistle to the church at Thessalonica, said, "Pray continually" (1 Thess. 5:17). Praying at all times means not only maintaining a constant attitude of prayer and taking advantage of the opportunity for open communication with God at any given moment, but it also means praying through matters without quitting. In Luke 18:1, as Jesus was sharing with his disciples the importance of persisting in prayer, he taught that we "should always pray and not give up."

Paul told the believers at Philippi to pray about everything. "Do not be anxious about anything, but in *every* situation…present your requests to God" (Phil. 4:6; emphasis mine).

We are also to pray for all Christians. In his instructions to the believers at Ephesus concerning spiritual warfare and their defense against Satan's attacks, Paul said, "Pray in the Spirit at all times and on every occasion. Stay alert and be persistent in your prayers for all believers everywhere" (Eph. 6:18, NLT).

We are also to pray, not just for all believers, but for all mankind, including those who have authority over us. To his pastoral protégé, Timothy, Paul wrote, "I urge, then, first of all, that petitions, prayers, intercession and thanksgiving be made for all people—for kings and all those in authority" (1 Tim. 2:1–2a).

We could go on. When it comes to the many commands we find in the Bible to pray, we have barely even scratched the surface. Clearly, it is paramount for us to remember that the reason we pray is because God has instructed us to do so. It is not a suggestion, a general guideline, or a responsibility left only to clergy and missionaries. It is not only a biblical mandate, an imperative that God has issued to every believer, but it is also an act of obedience on our part as we express our desire for and love to Him.

God's Way for Us to Receive

Each of us has needs. They can be material, physical, emotional, or spiritual in nature. Many of them are needs that we cannot (on our own) supply. Other times, there are needs we see in the lives of others that require supply, so we intercede with God on their behalf. Whichever the case, prayer is the way to receive supply, the way we ask God for essential things.

James, the half brother of Jesus, wrote to struggling Christ followers, "You do not have because you do not ask God" (Jas. 4:2). Jesus, too, taught us that prayer was the vehicle for receiving from God. In his Sermon on the Mount, he taught, "Ask and it will be given to you; seek and you will find; knock and the door will be opened to you. For everyone who asks receives" (Matt. 7:7–8a).

In Matthew 21, Jesus told his disciples, "If you believe, you will receive whatever you ask for in prayer" (Matt.

21:22), and in John 15:7, He declared, "If you remain in me and my words remain in you, ask whatever you wish, and it will be done for you" (John 15:7).

It doesn't take a nuclear physicist, a Nobel Prize winner, or a person with 180 IQ to see the one commonality to each of these verses that virtually leaps off the page—Ask!

It is the word *ask*. Ask. Ask. Ask. Again and again we see it. Why? Because asking is God's way for us to receive what we need.

In 1984, my older brother, Lon (now chairman of the music department at New Mexico State University) became the victim of departmental downsizing at Southwest Baptist University, the college in Missouri where he had been an instructor for two years. His contract for the next school year was not renewed, and without warning, his first collegiate job had been instantly taken away, like the proverbial rug that gets yanked out from under an unsuspecting man.

It was a tough blow to overcome, one that proved to be humbling. Lon began applying for other jobs at other schools, but with very little turnaround between the spring and fall semesters, open positions proved to be few and far between. He found rejection at every turn. He did everything he could to support his wife and baby daughter, even applying for a job at a local supermarket as a grocery sacker.

The summer break passed. It was mid-August when Lon suddenly got word of an opening at Paris Junior

College in Paris, Texas, for a position as director of the school's choral program.

He called to inquire about the job on a Wednesday from the church in west Texas where he and Dad had been leading a revival meeting together.

The PJC department chairman said, "Can you come tomorrow for an interview?"

Lon drove halfway across Texas that night and interviewed for the job on Thursday. On Friday, he was informed the position was his. He started the new job on Monday—the same day his wife, Susan, picked up his last paycheck from SBU!

Throughout his entire ordeal, my brother never stopped praying, never stopped trusting, never stopped humbly, fervently, persistently asking the Lord to provide for his needs. And when God did choose to move on his behalf, He did so in a spectacular way to demonstrate His own might and faithfulness. "You do not have because you do not ask God" (James 4:2).

God's Way for Us to Have Joy

As parents, we derive a tremendous amount of satisfaction from doing nice things for our children. It is one of the numerous ways we choose to express our love for them. These expressions can sometimes be simple things like a trip to the ice cream parlor or bringing home some bauble from a recent business trip. Other times, we may choose to lavish them with something more valuable.

When my oldest son, Ryan, was small, he loved it when I would purchase him superhero action figures or funny children's videos. (At the time of this writing, he is a senior engineering student in college, so his tastes have become inordinately more expensive.)

Oftentimes, we spell love T-I-M-E, and the greatest joy we can bring our children is quality togetherness. Other times it is the comforting hug in a moment of vulnerability when a hurting child needs no magic words of affirmation, but simply to be held.

Now consider what Jesus said:

> Which of you, if your son asks for bread, will give him a stone? Or if he asks for a fish, will give him a snake? If you, then, though you are evil, know how to give good gifts to your children, how much more will your Father in heaven give good gifts to those who ask him! (Matt. 7:9–11).

God, our heavenly Abba[2], is also a loving father who takes delight in his children and who desires to lavish joy upon us in ways too great to enumerate. Psalm 149:4 says that He takes delight in His people, and Psalm 37:23 (NLT)

---

2 Aramaic for "daddy."

states that He directs the steps of the godly. He delights in every detail of their lives.

But as much joy as He has already given us, how much more does God delight in the joy we receive when He chooses to answer our prayers?

The Lord, in His own words, makes it clear that prayer is one vehicle He uses to produce joy in our lives.

Jesus said, "Until now you have not asked for anything in my name. Ask and you will receive, and your *joy* will be complete" (John 16:24; emphasis mine).

Whether it is through His provision for our needs, His work in the lives of someone for whom we have been interceding, or simply the quiet wonder of a moment of communion as we bask in His presence, prayer is one of God's ways for us to have joy.

God's War against Skeptics

David wrote in Psalm 14:1, "The fool says in his heart, 'There is no God.'"

The theological term for a person who believes that nothing can be known of God's existence is an agnostic. Agnostic comes from the Greek words ἀ meaning *without*, and *gnōsis* meaning *knowledge*. In essence, the skeptic is a person without knowledge of God.

Yet few arguments could be more indisputable to critics and agnostics than the real-life effect of an answered prayer. There is, perhaps, no better scriptural example of this than that of the Prophet Elijah's confrontation with the prophets of Baal on Mount Carmel. This was essentially a contest to prove whose God was real and whose was false. After the prophets of Baal had spent the day dancing around the altar of sacrifice they had built, slashing themselves and fruitlessly beseeching their god Baal for a response, Elijah called upon Yahweh, the one true God.

> At the time of sacrifice, the Prophet Elijah stepped forward and prayed: "Lord, the God of Abraham, Isaac and Israel, let it be known today that you are God in Israel and that I am your servant and have done all these things at your command. Answer me, Lord, answer me, so these people will know that you, Lord, are God, and that you are turning their hearts back again." Then the fire of the Lord fell and burned up the sacrifice, the wood, the stones and the soil, and also licked up the water in the trench. When all the people saw this, they fell prostrate and cried, "The Lord—he is God! The Lord—he is God!" (1 Kgs. 18:36–39).

While Elijah's prayer to God over 2,800 years ago brought about the miraculous, it is my contention that God still delights to perform the supernatural today.

Case in point: Karla Bennett. A petite young lady, Karla had the sweetest singing voice and an even sweeter disposition. Karla not only lived in my hometown and went to my high school, but we were neighbors and members of the same church where my dad served as pastor.

She eventually married her high school sweetheart, Mark Betterton. After college, Mark embarked upon a career in coaching, which eventually led the two of them to Shawnee, Oklahoma, and Oklahoma Baptist University, where he coached basketball. It was while in Shawnee that Karla's health began to decline.

Soon came the shocking news that she had a brain tumor. Surgery was prescribed.

But Karla was a woman of faith who trusted God with her entire being, and she remembered James's instruction: "Is anyone among you sick? Let them call the elders of the church to pray over them and anoint them with oil in the name of the Lord. And the prayer offered in faith will make the sick person well" (Jas. 5:14–15).

So some godly men from her church in Shawnee were called to her home. They prayed fervently over her, asking that God would grant healing to her body.

The day for her surgery arrived. The surgeon ordered that one last scan of her brain be performed before they would proceed. You can imagine his amazement when the scan revealed that Karla's tumor had completely vanished!

The power of an answered prayer will have a huge impact in overcoming the argument of a skeptic.

God's Way to Have Peace

There is something in mankind's nature—perhaps pride—that creates the tendency to try to take matters into our own hands. But when left to our own devices, we are often incapable of overcoming difficulties that come our way. The inability to relinquish to God control of a situation (that we never really controlled to begin with) is called worry. Worry creates unnecessary anxiety. It is a lack of trust, the opposite of faith, and faith is something we must possess if we are ever going to please God (see Heb. 11:6).

So worrying does not please God.

This is an aspect of the human condition the Apostle Paul understood well. Let's revisit Philippians 4 for a moment, where he wrote to the church, "Do not be anxious about anything, but in every situation, by prayer and petition, with thanksgiving, present your requests to God. And the peace of God, which transcends all understanding, will guard your hearts and your minds in Christ Jesus" (Phil. 4:6–7).

Now, consider Jesus' teaching on this matter:

> Therefore I tell you, do not worry about your life, what you will eat or drink; or about your body, what you will wear. Is not life more than food, and the body more than clothes? Look at the birds of the air; they do not sow or reap or store away in barns, and yet your heavenly Father feeds them. Are you not much more valuable than they? Can any one of you by worrying add a single hour to your life?

> And why do you worry about clothes? See how the flowers of the field grow. They do not labor or spin. Yet I tell you that not even Solomon in all his splendor was dressed like one of these. If that is how God clothes the grass of the field, which is here today and tomorrow is thrown into the fire, will he not much more clothe you—you of little faith? So do not worry, saying, 'What shall we eat?' or 'What shall we drink?' or 'What shall we wear?' For the pagans run after all these things, and your heavenly Father knows that you need them. But seek first his kingdom and his righteousness, and all these things will be given to you as well. Therefore do not worry about tomorrow, for tomorrow will worry about itself. Each day has enough trouble of its own." (Matt. 6:25–34).

Likewise, what a wonderful blessing for us as well is Peter's instruction to "cast all your anxiety on him because he cares for you" (1 Pet. 5:7). Whether the need is exceedingly great or so small we mistakenly think it escapes God's notice, He cares. Moreover, as a loving father, He delights in having us declare our dependence on Him.

It was Sunday morning, February 26, 1995, about 6:30 a.m.. Kristi and I had just brought our firstborn child home from Norman Regional Hospital the night before, and as babies are prone to do, ours had kept us up that night. I vividly remember being rudely awakened that morning to the sound of a siren outside our bedroom window, followed by the sound of a doorbell. I groggily rolled out of bed, snatched the first item of clothing I could find (which happened to be Kristi's peach-colored bathrobe), and I stumbled to the door. When I opened it, the paramedic standing on my porch wanted me to describe our state of emergency. In my not-completely-conscious state, the only thought my addled brain could generate was, "What?"

My mother-in-law sheepishly emerged from the guest room to explain that a few moments earlier, while trying to make a call, she had accidentally pressed the E-1 button on our home phone. As it turns out, E-1 was preprogrammed to make 9-1-1 calls. She immediately realized her error and frantically hung up. But it was too late. Our number was already in the system.

But our experience was a fitting reminder of how impressive a state-of-the-art 9-1-1 emergency system really is. One need only dial the number and a display in front of the dispatcher pops up immediately with the appropriate phone number, address, and the name under which the number is listed. Additionally, all first responders—police, fire department, and paramedics—are listening in.

Thankfully, ours was a nonemergency situation (the only symptoms we were suffering from were sleep deprivation and the humiliation of being seen in my wife's clothes); however, there are times an emergency caller might be hysterical, unable to adequately articulate the problem in the frenzy of the moment. But thankfully, help is already on the way.

The point? Well, so it is with God.

When there is pain or anxiety in our lives, we often dial 9-1-1 prayers. Sometimes we are hysterical and do not know what to say. But God hears. He already knows our name and our exact circumstance. Fortunately for us, even when the anxiety is too great for us to voice our need, "the Spirit also helps our weakness; for we do not know how to pray as we should, but the Spirit Himself intercedes for us with groanings too deep for words" (Rom. 8:26, NASB).

Matthew Henry describes it this way:

> Though the infirmities of Christians are many and great, so that they would be overpowered if left to themselves, the Holy Spirit supports them. The Spirit, as an enlightening Spirit, teaches us what to pray for; as a sanctifying Spirit, works and stirs up praying graces; as a comforting Spirit, silences our fears, and helps us over all discouragements.[3]

Casting our cares upon God through prayer is a bonafide way to the kind of peace that banishes worry from our hearts and makes our broken roads easier to traverse.

---

3 Matthew Henry, *Matthew Henry's Concise Commentary On The Whole Bible* (Nashville: Thomas Nelson, Inc., 1977), 1080.

God's Way to Receive Power

Worry comes from wallowing in the knowledge that we are powerless to overcome troubling circumstances—particularly those along the broken road. Yet the power to overcome does exist. Jesus, in his parable of the Rich Young Ruler, emphasized man's inability to save himself. He stated, "With man this is impossible, but with God *all* things are possible" (Matt. 19:26; emphasis mine).

Paul wrote in Ephesians 3:20 that God "is able to do immeasurably more than all we ask or imagine, according to his power that is at work within us." What is the power that is at work within us? It is the power of the Holy Spirit, which resides within each believer in Christ (1 Cor. 6:19–20).

Of course, nowhere was the power of the Spirit more wondrously demonstrated than at Pentecost. The Scriptures tell us that when the Spirit came upon the apostles,

> All of them were filled with the Holy Spirit and began to speak in other tongues as the Spirit enabled them. Now there were staying in Jerusalem God-fearing Jews from every nation under heaven. When they heard this sound, a crowd came together in bewilderment, because each one heard their own language being spoken (Acts 2:4–6).

This supernatural manifestation of the Spirit's power in the apostles was amazing, but it should not have come as a surprise. Before Jesus ascended into heaven, He had already promised them: "You will receive power when the Holy Spirit comes on you; and you will be my witnesses in Jerusalem, and in all Judea and Samaria, and to the ends of the earth" (Acts 1:8).

So how do we receive the same power of the Holy Spirit? As a precursor, there is a brokenness, a surrendering of our will to God's, that must take place first. But the key step in experiencing the power of the Holy Spirit is to simply pray and ask. In Jesus' teaching on prayer in Luke 11, He stated, "How much more will your Father in heaven give the Holy Spirit to those who ask him!" (Luke 11:13).

Hebert Jackson, a former missionary, once told of a car he was assigned to use while on the mission field. Unfortunately, the standard-transmission car would not start on its own. What was required to get the engine running was a push to get it rolling, then a quick release of the clutch. Jackson pondered his problem and devised a plan. He often enlisted the neighborhood kids to push it, or parked it on a hill, or left it running—tricks he used for two years.

Health problems eventually forced him to leave the mission field. A new missionary arrived to begin the transition, and Dr. Jackson proudly explained his ingenious system for starting his car. But before he could finish, the new man began looking under the hood and said, "Here's your problem right here. Loose cable."

He gave it a twist, got in the car, turned the key, and the car roared to life.

For two years, trouble had become a needless routine. The power had always been there, ready to be put to work, but a poor connection prevented it. Likewise, only when we make a firm connection with God, through prayer, can His power flow fully through us.[4]

In his letter to the church at Ephesus, Paul spoke of God's "incomparably great power to us who believe. That power is the same as the mighty strength he exerted when he raised Christ from the dead and seated him at his right hand in the heavenly realms" (Eph. 1:19–20).

There is tremendous power in prayer—power to live, to serve, to love, and to overcome life's broken roads.

God's Wealth of Example

As a man or woman of God, who is your ultimate example in all things?

Christ is, of course! Both Jesus and the apostles set the standard for us with regard to being consistent in prayer. We would do well to follow that example.

---

4 Craig Brian Larson, Illustrations For Preaching And Teaching (Grand Rapids: Christianity Today/Baker House, 1993), 182.

We know that prayer was important to the apostles. When confronted with a problem in the fledgling first-century church involving inequitable treatment of certain widows in their congregation, they tasked godly men, the first deacons, to see to the needs in question so that they (the apostles) would be free to fully devote themselves continually "to prayer and to the ministry of the Word" (Acts 6:4). Prayer and teaching were the primary ministry of the first pastors, the apostles.

The example of the importance of prayer was also set for us in both the earthly and the heavenly ministry of Jesus Christ. Communion with God was a recurring activity for Him. In all, there are approximately thirty instances in the gospel records that mention Jesus' prayer life.

Mark 1:35 says, "Very early in the morning, while it was still dark, Jesus got up, left the house and went off to a solitary place, where he prayed." Jesus' travels and ministry were often exhausting. The previous day had been full of teaching, healing, and the casting out of many demonic spirits, yet Jesus deprived himself of much needed sleep in order to engage in much more needed prayer.

Not only was Jesus diligent about maintaining his prayer life, but he often devoted extended periods of time to prayer and communion with the Father. We find in Luke 6:12 that Jesus went out to a mountainside to pray, and spent the night praying to God. A similar instance occurs in Matthew 14:23.

One of Jesus' most impassioned prayers is found in John 17, where He not only seeks the Father's glory, but prays for his disciples, and then for all believers:

> I have given them the glory that you gave me, that they may be one as we are one—I in them and you in me—so that they may be brought to complete unity. Then the world will know that you sent me and have loved them even as you have loved me (John 17:22–23).

Those are powerful, beautiful words, but what is so glorious for believers today is, that Christ's ministry of prayer still continues in heaven. Even now, our risen Savior occupies a position of honor and power at the right hand of God, interceding with Him on our behalf. The writer of Hebrews said, "Because Jesus lives forever, his priesthood lasts forever. Therefore he is able, once and forever, to save those who come to God through him. He lives forever to intercede with God on their behalf" (Heb. 7:24–25, NLT).

Paul wrote in Romans 8:34, "Who then is the one who condemns? No one. Christ Jesus who died—more than that, who was raised to life—is at the right hand of God and is also interceding for us."

Ask yourself, "Why do I love Him?"

A likely answer is because He first loved you.

So why do we pray? Because Jesus prays for us. His devotion to prayer sets the standard for our own commitment to prayer.

The Paradigm of Prayer

Now that we have tackled the definition of prayer and the reasons to pray, the next obvious question for us to explore on the path to powerful prayer is, "How do we pray?"

One of Jesus' own disciples posed the question, requesting, "Lord, teach us to pray" (Luke 11:1). The instruction Jesus gave in response was poignant, practical, and powerful as he established for all believers seeking to approach the throne of God (Heb. 4:16) the pattern for prayer we fondly refer to as the Lord's Prayer, found in Matthew 6 and Luke 11.

The Matthew 6 record reads like this:

> Our Father in heaven, Your name be honored as holy. Your kingdom come. Your will be done on earth as it is in heaven. Give us today our daily bread. And forgive us our debts, as we also have forgiven our debtors. And do not bring us into temptation, but deliver us from the evil one. [For

> Yours is the kingdom and the power and the glory forever. Amen] (Matt. 6:9–13, HCSB)[1].

The reason Jesus gave us this instruction in Matthew 6 and Luke 11 is very simple. It is a blueprint for prayer. Jesus' disciple asked, "Lord, teach us to pray." It stands to reason though, that if Jesus' disciple had simply wanted a prayer, he would have said, "Lord, teach us a prayer." What he was truly seeking was for Jesus to teach them all the keys to successful prayer, and this is exactly what Jesus did. The prayer Jesus prayed gives us the structure for a prayer life that is powerful all the time, come prosperity or adversity.

In verse 9, Jesus says, "This is how you should pray," and the key aspects of powerful prayer that He illustrates are:

The Person

"Our Father," Jesus begins (v. 9). We are his children and we are to approach Him as our Father. It is important to understand this because prayer is meant for God's children. A nonbeliever can recite the Lord's Prayer and try to claim its promises all he wants, but for him, it is simply an empty recitation that holds no power. For a believer though, there is tremendous power in prayer since it was created as a means for God's children to fellowship with him.

The question is often asked, "Who do I pray to?"

---

1 Some manuscripts omit the bracketed text.

The simple answer is that we can pray to any of the three persons of the Trinity since all are God. He is one essence manifested in three persons, so anytime we pray to one person of the Trinity, we are praying to all; however, as children of God the Father, the simplest approach is to remember that we pray by the Spirit, to the Father, through the Son. Because we have Jesus as our great High Priest.

> Let us then approach the throne of grace with confidence, so that we may receive mercy and find grace to help us in our time of need (Heb. 4:16).

It is also important for us to bear in mind that we pray by the Spirit because, as we explored earlier, God is a spiritual being. When we speak to him, it must be from an outpouring of our heart, or more precisely, our spirit.[2]

Allow me to clarify this a bit.

We tend to think of prayer as a matter of the heart. In the context of prayer, the terms heart and spirit are interchangeable, at least according to our Judeo-Christian tradition. This interchangeability of terminology is described by Henri J. M. Nouwen in his book *The Way Of The Heart: Connecting With God Through Prayer, Wisdom, and Silence*.

---

2 See Chapter 1, *The Nature Of Prayer*.

> The heart, too, has its reasons and is the center of perception and understanding. Finally, the heart is the seat of the will: it makes plans and comes to good decisions. Thus the heart is the central and unifying organ of our personal life. Our heart determines our personality, and is therefore not only the place where God dwells, but also the place to which Satan directs his fiercest attacks. It is this heart that is the place of prayer. The prayer of the heart is a prayer that directs itself to God from the center of the person and thus affects the whole of our humanness.[3]

What Nouwen is really describing is the innermost part of our being, the part from which true prayer emanates—our spirit. Christians refer to it colloquially as the *heart*.

So believers pray from the innermost core of our being to the Father, through the Son, by the Spirit. Of course, the only problem with praying by the Spirit is that only a child of God can do so.

Why is this?

Ephesians 2:1 says that before coming to faith in Christ, our spirits were dead in our "transgressions and sins." Jesus said in John 3:6, "Flesh gives birth to flesh, but

---

3 Henri J.M. Nouwen, *The Way Of The Heart: Connecting With God Through Prayer, Wisdom and Silence* (New York: Random House Publishing, 1983), 74-75.

the Spirit gives birth to spirit." This is the experience that Christ called being born-again (John 3:3).

Jesus also stated in John 4:24 that "God is spirit, and his worshipers must worship in spirit and in truth." So it is by God's design that when we receive him through Christ, only then is our spirit enabled and equipped to commune with God by his Spirit in both worship and prayer.

It is also worthy of note that praying by the Spirit sometimes means praying in the Spirit as well. Paul wrote that "the Holy Spirit helps us in our weakness…the Spirit intercedes for the saints in accordance with God's will" (Rom. 8:26a, 27b, NLT).

I feel compelled to speak to the question of praying in the Spirit for a moment because there seems to some confusion about what this truly means.

What is praying in the Spirit?

Praying in the Spirit is mentioned three times in the Bible. Paul says, "So what shall I do? I will pray with my spirit, but I will also pray with my understanding; I will sing with my spirit, but I will also sing with my understanding" (1 Corinthians 14:15).

He exhorts believers to pray in the Spirit again in Ephesians 6 in the passage dealing with spiritual warfare. Then Jude, the half brother of Jesus, encourages believers to persevere in faith and love by "building yourselves up in your most holy faith and praying in the Holy Spirit" (Jude 20).

Many will associate praying in the Spirit with speaking in tongues, particularly since Paul's first use of the term is in the context of a discussion of the proper and improper use of the spiritual gift of tongues in the first-century church. But praying in the Spirit is really something much deeper than this.

The Greek wording that's translated into English as *pray in* means *with the help of* or *by means of*. So praying in the Spirit does not particularly refer to the words we say, so much as to how we pray them. By definition, praying in the Spirit is praying according to the Spirit's leading. It is praying for things the Spirit leads us to pray for. We don't always understand why the Spirit leads in these matters, but it is vital that we respond in obedience.

Several months ago, I woke up early one morning with an old high school friend and her husband weighing heavy on my mind. Mind you, I have not seen Tina in more than thirty years, and I have never even met her husband, Todd. Though I had read on a social media site that Todd had been going through some career upheaval, a year or so had already passed. It had been weeks since I had even had a passing thought of my friend. Yet the first thing on my mind when I rolled out of bed that particular day was the strong urge to pray for Tina and Todd, specifically for his job situation. So I did.

You can imagine the overwhelming confirmation that something (more to the point, someone) bigger than me was at work when a couple of hours later I logged on to Facebook to read Tina's request for prayer for God's grace and blessing for Todd as he headed to a vitally important job interview that day.

At the time, I had no clue why I was supposed to pray, but God knew, and his Holy Spirit led me in what I should pray for. That is praying in the Spirit.

We don't always know what to pray or how to say it, but God's Spirit is already at work, taking care of such things. Sadly, because of a perceived lack of word skills, some believers suffer from the mistaken notion that they cannot pray, but as we've seen, our communion with the Father in prayer is, at its core, a spiritual experience, not merely a verbal one. We pray to God, through Christ, by means of the Spirit.

The Praise

In the Lord's Prayer, Jesus said, "Your name be honored as holy" (v. 9) and "Yours is the…glory" (v. 13). Most translations use the word *hallowed* which means *holy*. Jesus is teaching us to praise God for his many wonderful attributes.

And why not?

Psalm 22:3 says God inhabits the praise of his people. When we pray, praise should be the first thing upon our lips. None of the rest of our prayer really matters if we cannot pray with God's glory as our first and greatest priority.

After all, that is why we exist—to bring glory to our Lord in all things.

Why should prayer be any different?

"You are holy, God—infinite in power, wisdom, righteousness and love—and I pray that you will live through me to bring glory to your name today."

We ought to pray something like that daily, because we exist to extol His name.

What better way to begin our prayers than by thanking and praising God for all the wonderful things He is! He is a mighty, holy God, everlasting Father, Creator, Shepherd, Healer, Provider, Savior, Teacher, Encourager, Friend, soon-coming King, and so much more. He is our all-in-all. We should praise Him for that.

Some Bible manuscripts include this phrase in verse 13 at the end of the Lord's Prayer: "For Yours is the kingdom and the power and the glory forever."

Is there a more fitting way to end a prayer than just as we began—by giving God the passionate praise He deserves?

The writers of Psalms knew how to do that. The word *praise* appears in the Psalms approximately 176 times.

Many Puritan believers knew how to do that as well.

Listen to this excerpt from a collection of Puritan prayers called The Valley of Vision: "There is one thing that deserves my greatest care, that calls forth my ardent desires.

That is, that I may answer the great end for which I am made—to glorify thee who hast given me being."[4]

While the language may seem archaic to us, the overflow of praise to the Creator from the abundance of a thankful heart seems ubiquitous in true believers from all ages.

Powerful prayer overflows with praise. Why? Because praise is an expression of faith. It is a way that God's children give Him predetermined thanks for prayers yet to be answered.

The Purpose

"*Your* kingdom come, *your will* be done," Jesus said (emphasis mine).

We also exist for God's will and purpose. We need to acknowledge that God has a purpose and a plan for our lives and surrender to His leading, because "prayer is the means by which we can know God and His will for our lives."[5]

As we previously discussed, prayer is not an exercise where we bend God's will to fit ours.[6]

E. Stanley Jones once astutely observed,

4 *The Valley of Vision: A Collection of Puritan Prayers & Devotions*, ed. by Arthur Bennett (Carlisle: Banner Of Truth Trust, 1975), 13.

5 Ronnie W. Floyd, *How To Pray: Developing An Intimate Relationship With God* (Nashville: Word Publishing/Thomas Nelson, Inc., 1999), Kindle e-book.

6 See Chapter 1, *The Nature Of Prayer*.

> Prayer is surrender—surrender to the will of God and cooperation with that will. If I throw out a boat hook from a boat and catch hold of the shore and pull, do I pull the shore to me, or do I pull myself to the shore? Prayer is not pulling God to my will, but the aligning of my will to the will of God.[7]

Prayer is seeking God's will and following it. We should pray in the satisfaction of knowing that God's will is determined with our best interests in mind (see Rom. 8:28).

Consider these scriptures that relate prayer to God's will (I have added emphasis for additional clarity):

- 1 John 5:14 says, "This is the confidence we have in approaching God: that if we ask anything *according to his will*, He hears us."
- Jesus said in John 15:7, "If you remain in me and *my words remain in you*, ask whatever you wish, and it will be given you."
- James, the half brother of Jesus, wrote, "When you ask, you do not receive, because you ask with wrong motives" (James 4:3). (James knew that while is it vital to our prayer lives to pray in accordance with

7 E. Stanley Jones, *A Song Of Ascents: A Spiritual Autobiography*, quoted in Charles R. Swindoll, *Swindoll's Ultimate Book Of Illustrations & Quotes* (Nashville: Thomas Nelson, Inc., 1998), 453.

God's will, praying from outside of it brings a very different result.)[8]

We find another model prayer in 2 Samuel 7:18–29 that teaches us the importance of praying God's will. In the events leading up to David's prayer, we find that the Ark of the Covenant has no permanent home.

David tells Nathan the prophet, "Here I am, living in a house of cedar, while the ark of God remains in a tent" (2 Sam. 7:2). So he arrives at the conclusion that he should build a temple for the Lord. Initially, Nathan agrees with David, but later receives a word from the Lord instructing him that his plan has been rejected by God.

Nathan, on God's behalf, announced to David in 1 Chronicles 22:9, "You have shed much blood and have fought many wars. You are not to build a house for my Name, because you have shed much blood on the earth in my sight."

The responsibility for building the temple would fall to Solomon. David chose to be obedient to God's instruction in this matter because, ultimately, seeing God's will done was far more important to him than seeing his own desires carried out.

But because David made his desires subordinate to God's, the Lord pronounced a blessing upon David, promising to give him rest from his enemies, and saying:

---

8 More on this in Chapter 6, *The Waiting Of Prayer.*

> The LORD declares to you that the LORD himself will establish a house for you: When your days are over and you rest with your ancestors, I will raise up your offspring to succeed you, your own flesh and blood, and I will establish his kingdom…Your house and your kingdom will endure forever before me; your throne will be established forever (2 Sam. 7:11–12, 16).

Then in gratitude and humility, David begins to pray:

> Who am I, Sovereign LORD, and what is my family, that you have brought me this far? And as if this were not enough in your sight, Sovereign LORD, you have also spoken about the future of the house of your servant—and this decree, Sovereign LORD, is for a mere human! What more can David say to you? For you know your servant, Sovereign LORD. For the sake of your word and *according to your will*, you have done this great thing and made it known to your servant (2 Sam. 7:18–21; emphasis mine).

God acted according to His own purposes, not David's, and saw fit to bless David, who continues in v. 22, "How great you are, Sovereign LORD! There is no one like you, and there is no God but you, as we have heard with our own ears."

David had come full circle from his declaration of desire to build God a temple to acknowledgement that God had already done everything for him, and for Israel

(vv. 23–24). In verse 27, he says, "LORD Almighty, God of Israel, you have revealed this to your servant, saying, 'I will build a house for you.' So your servant has found courage to pray this prayer to you."

In short, instead of building God a house, God is building David a house!

David came to realize that God's blessings and His desires are truly best, so all that he could do at this point was agree with God! He declares, "Keep forever the promise you have made…do as you promised" (v. 25). "Bless the house of your servant that it may continue forever in your sight" (v. 29).

After reading David's prayer, we must ask ourselves if there can be any prayer more powerful and worthy than the prayer that agrees with God's will.

Theologian Thomas Hauff puts it this way: "The best things to suggest to God are those that at most are expressions of what He's already made clear He wants from us."[9]

In David's case, his obedience brought him into line with God's will.

Praying in submission to God's will might sound something like, "God, I surrender to your Lordship today. I

---

9 Thomas R. Hauff, *When God Says No: Reshaping Prayer And Learning To Listen* (Eugene: Resource Publications/Wipf and Stock Publishers, 2011), 294.

bow to your will and pray that you break mine. Make your desires my desires."

The Petition

One of the reasons we pray is so that God will meet our needs.[10] Here in verse 11 of Matthew 6, Jesus said, "Give us today our daily bread."

This simple statement is symbolic of our requests for God to meet all of our needs. The Apostle Paul reminds us in Philippians 4:19 that "my God will meet all your needs according to the riches of His glory in Christ Jesus."

How many times do God's children go without because they simply fail to petition their heavenly Father to supply their needs?

"If you need bread, ask God for a loaf. If you need a job, ask Him for a job. If you need a house, ask Him for a house."[11]

God's Word is full of promises that He will supply our need. His desires to lavish blessing upon His children. He is just waiting for us to humble ourselves, admit our dependence on Him, and ask.

We must not forget, however, that petition means more than simply praying for ourselves and our own needs. As

10 See Chapter 2, *The Necessity Of Prayer*.

11 Adrian Rogers, *What Every Christian Ought To Know* (Nashville: Broadman & Holman Publishers, 2005), 219.

fervently as we seek God's provision for our own needs, we should also make intercession for other people and ask God to fill their needs, too.

Just like a little child with a boo-boo who needs a father's attention, our God is a loving Father who wants his children to come to Him with our concerns. 1 Peter 5:7 says, "Cast all your anxiety on him because he cares for you."

I want to take some time to more fully explore the concept of intercession, here, because the Apostle Paul gives us a wonderful example of another type of intercession in his prayer for the Ephesian believers.

Typically, when we pray on behalf of another individual, the specific needs we address might include prayers for healing from sickness, for God to supply some material need, or for God to otherwise improve another's circumstances. Obviously, if the person for whom we pray is not a believer, then typically we will pray for his or her salvation. These types of prayers are often necessary, but in Ephesians, Paul shows us—in what is not so much a model prayer like that of Jesus in Matthew 6, but more an explanation of how he prays—that there is a prayer on behalf of others that is much deeper and more lasting than a request for a change in someone's current circumstance. Listen to what he writes:

> I do not cease to give thanks for you when I remember you in my prayers. 17 I pray that the God of our Lord Jesus Christ, the Father of glory, may give you spiritual wisdom and revelation in your growing

> knowledge of him, 18—since the eyes of your heart have been enlightened—so that you may know what is the hope of his calling, what is the wealth of his glorious inheritance in the saints, 19 and what is the incomparable greatness of his power toward us who believe (Ephesians 1:16–19a, NET).

There are a number of things we learn here from Paul, not the least of which is that Paul prays for them continually. In verse 16, he says "I do not cease to...remember you in my prayers."

But what is Paul asking for? Verses 17–18 reveal both the answer and the depth of Paul's prayer life. Over and above the temporal concerns of daily life, Paul is continually asking God to grant the Ephesians knowledge of Him, and that, as a by-product of such knowledge, they understand some vital elements of their life in Him. This is a practice that every believer should embrace and perform on behalf of fellow Christians.

Hauff writes:

> We are praying for things that might benefit them [other believers] externally, how they act, but would hinder them internally, how they think and believe. I believe that if we were to prioritize the two, the internal needs far outweigh the external ones.[12]

---

12 Thomas R. Hauff, *When God Says No: Reshaping Prayer And Learning To Listen* (Eugene: Resource Publications/Wipf and Stock Publishers, 2011), 274.

If we truly desire to make a lasting impact for the Kingdom of God, then a frequent element in our daily prayers should be requests for God to: 1) Give others a spirit of wisdom and revelation, and 2) that the eyes of their hearts be enlightened so that they can fully understand the blessed hope of their calling.

The Pardon

Jesus continued in Matthew 6, "Forgive us our debts as we also have forgiven our debtors" (v. 12). The parallel passage in Luke 11 reads, "Forgive us our sins, for we also forgive everyone who sins against us."

We should be ever mindful that when we confess our sin that God forgives us the same way we forgive others. If we harbor unforgiveness toward others, God will not forgive us. Jesus makes this clear: "if you do not forgive men their sins, your Father will not forgive your sins" (Matthew 6:15).

Confessions of our sin is vital to an effective prayer life.[13] 1 John 1:9 states, "If we confess our sins, He is faithful and just and will forgive us our sins and purify us from all unrighteousness."

After the confession of individual sins, the words of King David in Psalm 51:10 become a soothing balm to heal

13 We will discuss this thought in more detail in Chapter 6, *The Waiting Of Prayer*.

our self-inflicted wounds: "Create in me a pure heart, O God, and renew a steadfast spirit within me." Each day, we should ask God for what scholars call tabula rasa, a clean slate, because a pure heart and a fresh start is necessary to enjoy refreshed fellowship with the Lord.

The old saying is true. Confession really is good for the soul, a key step toward the restoration of intimacy with God.

The Protection

"Lead us not into temptation, but deliver us from the evil one," Jesus said in verse 13. Here, He is teaching us to pray for God to keep us safe from two things: our own flesh and our adversary, Satan.

First, let us discuss temptation. We often find in the Christian life that it is necessary to protect our hearts in order to prevent ourselves from giving in to temptation. Psalm 26 says we can do that by walking continually in the "truth," meaning the Word of God. That is how He leads us away from temptation. When our minds are inundated with the Word, it will trickle down into our hearts and flow out into our lives. An ear that is tuned to the voice of the Holy Spirit, coupled with a healthy knowledge of the scriptures, will equip us to recognize sin for what it is and to sidestep the land mines that our own flesh will place in our path.

There is a second entity from whom we need protection: Satan. He is an enemy who knows that there is power in prayer, so he and his demons will try anything and everything to hinder us from praying. If this occurs, we are defeated before we even start. It is not that Satan is interested in us, personally. He is not. The truth is that Satan hates God and he wants to hurt God by hurting the ones God loves—His children.

So we do sometimes need protection from the "evil one." John 10:10 tells us that our adversary is a thief who comes to "steal, kill and destroy," but later, in verse 28, the Lord, our shepherd, promises, "no one can snatch them out of my hand."

Psalm 61—most likely written by David as he fled from his son, Absalom—describes God as our strong tower against the foe. David hungers to "take refuge in the shelter" of God's wings.

In addition to the pattern Jesus established for us in the Lord's Prayer, we also take this opportunity to elaborate on two other important facets of prayer that Jesus, and scripture, bring to light.

The Pause

Jesus, in a preamble to the Lord's Prayer, established the importance of a place of solitude to shut out the cacophony of worldly distraction and to quell the desire to gain validation by only praying publicly. In verses 5-6 of chapter 6, Jesus says:

> And when you pray, do not be like the hypocrites, for they love to pray standing in the synagogues and on the street corners to be seen by men. I tell you the truth, they have received their reward in full. 6 But when you pray, go into your room, close the door and pray to your Father, who is unseen. Then your Father, who sees what is done in secret, will reward you.

It is frequently in the quiet of these Psalm 46:10, "be-still-and-know-that-I-am-God" moments that we best hear the voice of God speaking to us—oftentimes through His Word, but also through the voice of the Holy Spirit.

"If you want to capture someone's attention, whisper." That was the 1976 tagline for Nuance perfume. I chuckle now as I think back on those silly TV commercials. But even though the sole intent was to sell the aromatic product, there is actually truth in that slogan. Sometimes a gentle whisper can speak louder than a screaming lunatic, especially when it comes in the calm after a storm.

Case in point: the prophet Elijah. In 1 Kings 19, God captured Elijah's attention with what verse 12 calls "a gentle whisper." In that still, secluded quiet moment, God blessed Elijah by assuaging the fears he had entertained as he fled for his life from the wicked Queen Jezebel. In the midst of Elijah's weariness and trouble, God created a perfect moment in time in which Elijah could commune with him and be recharged to go on for God.[14]

Henri J.M. Nouwen emphasizes the need for not only solitude, but a solitude that is enhanced by silence. This silence is an extraordinary silence. It is not merely "emptiness and silence, but fullness and presence, not the human silence of embarrassment, shame or guilt, but the divine silence in which love rests secure."[15]

Whoever coined the phrase "silence is golden," must have possessed gifted insight. We all need those moments, free of distraction, when we can turn our attention to nothing else than the presence of God. How wondrous those moments can be.

With four exuberant kids in my house and seldom a tranquil moment, it can be difficult to slip away and find quiet time with God. So I often spend time in prayer and the Word first thing in the morning when I get to my office. However, my office—with its paper-thin walls—is located on the second floor of a Christian school that is bustling with excitement and activity, which is, admittedly, a good thing. But sometimes those quiet moments are hard to come by when competing against the stampeding of

---

14 We will study Elijah's experience in 1 Kings 19 in more detail in Chapter 7, *The Wilderness Of Purpose.*

15 Henri J.M. Nouwen, *The Way Of The Heart: Connecting With God Through Prayer, Wisdom and Silence* (New York: Random House Publishing, 1983), 49.

middle schoolers who like to run down the hall outside my west wall; or the sounds of Mandarin wafting through from the classroom on the other side of my east wall; or the periodic "ziiiiiit, ziiiiiit, ziiiiiit" of the motorized paper towel dispenser in the boys' bathroom beyond the north wall; or the sounds of my assistant's phone conversations just outside my south wall. Needless to say, I, for one, have come to greatly appreciate the quiet moments and settings when and where I can steal away with God.

Still, one of the most vital aspects of our personal prayer lives that is overlooked by many believers is the time of silence—not just the silence when we pray, but the silence when we listen and meditate. We often devote a great deal of time pouring our hearts out to God, only to walk away after the final "amen," instead of allowing time for silent solitude and the opportunity for the voice of the Holy Spirit to speak to us in return.

The Persistence

There is another "p" for us to remember in the paradigm of prayer: persistence. Both experiential witness as well as the scriptures—including Jesus' teachings—tell us that persistence pays, in everyday life and, yes, in spiritual matters, too. This is especially true in our prayer life, and is of utmost importance to us when we are walking a broken road—which is why we will "table" this part of our discussion for now in order to devote a much more considerable amount of attention to this subject in Chapter 5, The Persistence of Prayer.

The person, the praise, the purpose, the petition, the pardon, the protection, the pause, and the persistence. This is Jesus' paradigm of prayer, and while these labels are catchy and easy to remember, Christ never intended for our prayer life to be overly formulaic—following the same order and form every time. Otherwise, it might one day become no more effective than the vain repetition, the "babble," Jesus spoke of in verse 7. This sample prayer simply provides a basic guideline to follow in our daily lives, and it also gives us insight into just how powerful, intimate and dynamic our prayer life can be.

The Prerequisites of Prayer

In the previous chapters, we have explored what prayer is, why it is necessary, and we've examined its basic blueprint. But how do we take everything we have learned thus far and put it to work? How do we create a prayer life that is powerful? To that end, we will examine twelve aspects of an effective prayer life in the pages ahead.

Pray with God's Desires

The first step in our 12-step plan to more effective prayer is to understand that the end goal is not our desired result, but God's.

Thomas R. Hauff declares that our focus in prayer begins and ends with God: "I cannot emphasize this enough. Your needs are important. Your friends' needs are important. The world's needs are important. But no needs are as important as God himself…and the sooner we come to terms with this truth, the sooner our prayer lives will begin to be truly effective."[1]

Mankind was created for God's good pleasure. There is no higher goal. Every fiber of our being, every aspect of our lives should revolve around this truth. The Apostle Paul said, "whatever you do, do it all for the glory of God" (1 Corinthians 10:31, emphasis mine).

Doing all for the glory of God, however, includes praying according to His will, not our own. The Apostle John wrote, "This is the confidence we have in approaching God: that if we ask anything according to His will, he hears us" (1 John 5:14–15).

The operative words are "according to His will." How do we know how to pray according to God's will? There are a number of ways God may choose to reveal His will to us: through the counsel of a Christian brother, through God's providence in our circumstances, through signs or miracles, or through the voice of the Holy Spirit. More often than not, however, God chooses to use wisdom and the Word to show us His desires.

So if we are going to pray according His will, then we require His wisdom. Thankfully, God is lavish in this regard. James wrote, "If any of you lacks wisdom, you should ask God, who gives generously to all without finding fault,

---

1 Thomas R. Hauff, *When God Says No: Reshaping Prayer And Learning To Listen* (Eugene: Resource Publications/Wipf and Stock Publishers, 2011), 311.

and it will be given to you" (James 1:5). James wrote this to people who were going through trials, so his counsel is apropos for those of us walking the broken road.

James goes on to say, "But when you ask, you must believe and not doubt, because the one who doubts is like a wave of the sea, blown and tossed by the wind" (James 1:6). So praying according to God's will not only means asking for wisdom, so that we can know His will, but also asking with a firm faith so that we can fully trust God's will.

Having a firm grasp of the Bible also helps to ensure that we are praying in a manner consistent with the Father's desires, since His will is most often revealed through Scripture. God's will never contradicts His Word, so we must learn to pray in harmony with it in order to pray for that which He desires.

Thankfully, in those instances when we honestly do not know what to pray for, as God's children we can lean on the Holy Spirit for assistance. Paul taught us that "the Spirit intercedes on behalf of the saints according to God's will" (Romans 8:27).

Pray in Right Standing

According to James, "The prayer of a righteous man is powerful and effective" (James 5:16), and the Apostle Peter, quoting from Psalm 34, said, "For the eyes of the Lord are on the righteous and his ears are attentive to their prayer, but the face of the Lord is against those who do evil" (1 Peter 3:12).

It was the prayer of a righteous man, Daniel, who faced the imminent prospect of becoming a snack for ferocious felines, that moved God to shut the mouths of lions.

In the wilderness of the Sinai it was Moses' right standing with God that stayed the Lord's hand of judgment against the children of Israel (Exodus 16–17).

Solomon, in all his wisdom, declared that "the prayer of the upright pleases Him" (Proverbs 15:8).

What do all these examples have in common? Righteousness. It is our right standing with God—coupled with Jesus' high priesthood—that qualifies us to approach Him in prayer. However, to grasp the fullness of what the scripture is teaching us here, it is necessary to differentiate between two types of righteousness.

Genesis 15:6 says, "Abraham believed God and it was credited to him as righteousness" (see also Romans 4:3,22–23; Galatians 3:6; James 2:23). What is significant is that it is a righteousness that is also extended to us, Abraham's descendants of faith.

The Greek word that is translated as "credited" (sometimes as "accounted" or "imputed") in Romans, Galatians and James is *logizomai*, which is an accounting term. Simply put, because of our faith, God has deposited Christ's own righteousness into our lives' accounts. While we still sin, and thus are not practically righteous, because we are—as Paul has said 85 times in his epistles—"in Christ," we are positionally righteous because of our faith.

While God desires practical righteousness from us as we walk in obedience to Him, without the positional righteousness afforded us by Christ, our prayers would be worthless.

Pray for Cleansing

The Bible says, "Whoever conceals their sins does not prosper, but the one who confesses and renounces them finds mercy" (Proverbs 28:13). It is vital that we make sure we have no unconfessed sin in our hearts when we pray. This would be an unmistakable impediment to effective prayer. How blessed we are, however, that "If we confess our sins, He is faithful and just and will forgive us our sins and purify us from all unrighteousness" (1 John 1:9).[2]

Pray with Commitment

Prayer is something believers are meant to do "continually" (1 Thessalonians 5:17). Unfortunately, we have a tendency to resist the development of a consistent prayer life. Paul understood this struggle with what the Bible calls "the flesh." He wrote, "For I know that nothing good dwells in me, that is, in my flesh. For I have the desire to do what is

---

2 The need for confession and cleansing is something we will discuss at length in Chapter 6, *The Waiting Of Prayer*.

right, but not the ability to carry it out. For I do not do the good I want, but the evil I do not want is what I keep on doing" (Romans 7:18–19, ESV).

The scripture also says this of Jesus: "Then he returned to his disciples and found them sleeping. 'Couldn't you men keep watch with me for one hour?' he asked Peter. 'Watch and pray so that you will not fall into temptation. The spirit is willing, but the flesh is weak'" (Matthew 26:40–41).

An uncommitted prayer life is a powerless prayer life. If we want to be certain our prayers are effective, we must go about the business of prayer fervently and persistently. In fact, this entire systematic exploration of prayer, from intro to endnotes, is built upon the premise that it is the power of persistent prayer that enables us to walk the broken roads of life. [3]

Pray with Confidence

If we are going to pray with supreme confidence, especially when limping through the wilderness, then there is one truth we should remember above all others: All prayer should be prayed in the name of Jesus! We do this, not only because He is our High Priest, our conduit to God, but also because that is how Jesus taught us to pray.

In John 14:12–14, Jesus said, "I tell you the truth, anyone who has faith in me will do what I have been doing.

3 Chapter 5, *The Persistence Of Prayer*, is dedicated to this very concept.

He will do even greater things than these, because I am going to the Father. And I will do whatever you ask in my name, so that the Son may bring glory to the Father. You may ask me for anything in my name, and I will do it" (emphasis mine).

In John 15:16, Jesus said, "You did not choose me, but I chose you and appointed you to go and bear fruit—fruit that will last. Then the Father will give you whatever you ask in my name" (emphasis mine).

In the next chapter, John 16, Jesus stated that "In that day you will no longer ask me anything. I tell you the truth, my Father will give you whatever you ask in my name. Until now you have not asked for anything in my name. Ask and you will receive, and your joy will be complete" (John 16:23–24, emphasis mine).

We also pray in the name of Jesus because it is the only name that is worthy. In Spiritual Secrets of George Müller, Müller, a British pastor and evangelist of the 19th century, explains it this way:

> We do not ask on account of our own goodness or merit, but as the Scripture expresses it, 'In the name of the Lord Jesus Christ.'...It means that just as by faith in the Lord Jesus Christ we shall stand before God at the last, so it is now in approaching unto God in prayer. If we desire to have our petitions answered, we must come to him, not in our own name, but as sinners who trust in Jesus, who by

> faith in His name are united to the blessed risen Lord, who have become, through trusting in Him, members of that body of which He is the head… Therefore on the ground of our goodness we cannot expect to have our prayers answered. But Jesus is worthy, and for His sake we may have our prayers answered.[4]

It is also true that the name of Jesus grants us authority. As such, his name should never be something we just tag on the end of our prayers as a matter of routine. We should always pray in the name of Jesus, not only because Jesus taught us such, and because His name is the only worthy one, but also because of the authority the name commands.

The Apostle Paul wrote in Colossians 3:17, "And whatever you do, whether in word or deed, do it all in the name of the Lord Jesus, giving thanks to God the Father through him."

It stands to reason that, if we are going to do all—including praying—in the name of Jesus, then it also means living in a manner that would meet with His approval. If bearing the name of Jesus means approval as well as authority, we must also be mindful of the fact that our prayer will not have Jesus' authority if it does not first have

---

4 *Spiritual Secrets of George Müller*, compiled by Roger Steer (Wheaton: Harold Shaw Publishers/OMF Books, 1985), 87-88.

His approval. So it is imperative that we pray in a manner consistent with His character and with scripture.

Pray with Expectancy

The writer of Hebrews once penned these words: "Without faith it is impossible to please God, because anyone who comes to him must believe that he exists and that he rewards those who earnestly seek him" (Hebrews 11:6). Having an effective prayer life is problematic without significant faith, too.

We serve a God who is omnipotent, so "Is anything too hard for the LORD?" (Genesis 18:14). No, because "with God all things are possible" (Matthew 19:26). As a result, there is no need, problem or request that is ever too big for God—our sustainer, shepherd, Father and architect of the universe—to handle. Such knowledge ought to fill us with a sense of expectancy when we pray.

Jesus said: "Have faith in God. Truly I tell you, if anyone says to this mountain, 'Go, throw yourself into the sea,' and does not doubt in their heart but believes that what they say will happen, it will be done for them. Therefore I tell you, whatever you ask for in prayer, believe that you have received it, and it will be yours" (Mark 11:22–24).

The Apostle John wrote: "This is the confidence we have in approaching God: that if we ask anything according to His will, He hears us. And if we know that He hears us—

whatever we ask—we know that we have what we asked of Him" (1 John 5:14–15, emphasis mine).

In spite of these promises, for some, any sort of faith is hard to come by—much less faith that God will answer prayer. Like the father of the demon possessed boy in Mark 9, there are times we need to be transparent with God and confess, "I do believe; help me overcome my unbelief!" (Mark 9:24). To paraphrase: Lord, I have faith, but help me to increase it!

For others, we stumble over the belief that somehow faith is supposed to bring emotion. Greg Frizzell writes: "It is vital to remember that faith must be a 'choice' and more than a mere 'feeling.' There will be many times you must choose to believe and keep praying in spite of consequences and feelings to the contrary."[5]

I love the way that pastor and Bible scholar Stephen Olford once put it: "Pray when you feel like it. Pray when you don't feel like it. Pray until you feel like it!"[6]

Whenever you pray, pray with confidence that God will answer.

---

5 Gregory R. Frizzell, *How To Develop A Powerful Prayer Life* (Memphis: Master Design Ministries, 1999), 44-45.

6 Dr. Stephen Olford, *The Dynamics of Anointed Expository Preaching: Question And Answer #2* (Memphis: Olford Ministries International), audio lecture.

Pray Specifically

To truly see God anoint our prayers, there are a good number of things we need to be specific about, including our intercession, our confession, our thanksgiving and more. With this specificity in mind, Thomas Mauff writes:

> Without concrete prayer requests, we are never forced to really identify what we are talking about. There is nothing like being specific in your prayers to show you whether your prayer life is really in tune with God's desires. If your specific requests are being met concretely, then you can be assured you are on God's page. If not, then it's time to reassess your program.[7]

Paul began the book of Ephesians with these words: "Praise be to the God and Father of our Lord Jesus Christ, who has blessed us in the heavenly realms with every spiritual blessing in Christ" (Ephesians 1:3, emphasis mine). Paul's praise reminds me of an old hymn we sang in my youth. "Count your blessings, name them one by one. Count your blessings, see what God has done."[8]

---

7 Thomas R. Hauff, *When God Says No: Reshaping Prayer And Learning To Listen* (Eugene: Resource Publications/Wipf and Stock Publishers, 2011), 311.

8 Johnson Oatman, Jr./Edwin O. Excell, "Count Your Blessings," *Baptist Hymnal* (Nashville: Lifeway Worship, 2008), 585.

In 2009, I was walking a broken road of my own, one pitted with very difficult and disappointing events, a road that would take nearly three years of struggling and searching to navigate. In February of that year, I had willfully chosen to leave the Baptist church I pastored in Lubbock, Texas in order to spare that body of believers from the undesirable division that loomed large in the church's future. Had the Spirit not led me to walk away, this ugly in-fighting would have been the inevitable consequence of unresolvable conflict created by some unrepentant men whose sole agenda was to see their pastor removed from his position of leadership.

Leaving was a radical choice in the eyes of some. To simply resign from a job with the looming specter of unemployment in the midst of the worst recession America had seen in decades seemed ludicrous. But then something amazing happened. My wife, Kristi, encouraged me to start a daily journal of all the blessings God was pouring out on my life. After a few months of logging the things God had done in the wake of my departure, both small and monumental, I began to see that God was pouring out buckets of blessings upon me and my family! Had I not learned to thank Him specifically, I would not have seen what He was up to, and, as a result, would not have gained a new appreciation for my heavenly Father.

Not only should we be specific in our thanks, but we also need to train ourselves to be specific in our intercession.

When we pray on behalf of others, it is far too easy to launch blanket requests like: "Lord, bless them" or "we lift him up to you, Lord." "Just be with her, Father." I know that God knows the intent of our hearts, but to experience real power in prayer, why not ask God to do something very specific? Instead of asking God to "be with" Gail or to "bless her" in the wake of being served with divorce papers, perhaps it would be more effective to pray something like:

> Father,
>
> I come humbly before your throne on behalf of my friend and sister, Gail, acknowledging that only you can ease the deep hurt and confusion she's suffering. I know that you are with her because your Spirit dwells within her. But I ask that you would make your presence known to her in a supernatural way, today, either by the moving of your Holy Spirit or by bringing encouragers into her life to offer comfort and wise counsel. Lord, I pray that your actions on her behalf and the ministry of your Holy Spirit would work to heal the betrayal she feels. Your Word says that you will never leave us or forsake us. I ask that you would remind her that you are always faithful, and that you are her healer, restorer and rewarder. Please grant divine favor to her as she struggles through the difficult days ahead. In Jesus' name I pray, amen.

Equal in importance to specific intercession is specific confession. Often in corporate worship or small group settings we will hear someone pray something like: "Lord, forgive us our shortcomings," or "forgive us where we have failed you," or "grant pardon for our weaknesses." In fact, these phrases are uttered so often, they have inadvertently become a part of our "Christians" lexicon.

Sadly, none of these is a true admission of sin. Sin is not a mistake, a failing, a weakness or shortcoming. Using such labels is an attempt—either consciously or subconsciously—to sugarcoat our sin. In our confession to God, can we not simply—to borrow a phrase from Aristophanes—"call a spade a spade"?

Sin is sin. It can be defined as "actions by which humans rebel against God, miss His purpose for their life, and surrender to the power of evil rather than to God," but more concisely put, sin is rebellion against God. Why would we call it anything else?[9]

Perhaps it is because we have mimicked worldly habits. The world, too, employs the same mechanism we Christians do to make morally reprehensible behavior seem more palatable.

---

9 Billy E. Simmons, *Holman Illustrated Bible Dictionary* , ed. Trent C. Butler (Nashville: Holman Bible Publishers, 2003), 1505.

"She chose to terminate the pregnancy." No, she willingly took the life of a child.[10]

"He had an extramarital fling." Yet "fling" is far too flippant a description for the type of betrayal and hurt caused by adultery, is it not?

"They misappropriated funds." No, they stole from the company!

If we want to be serious about experiencing God's cleansing, and the renewed power it brings to our prayer life, then we need to be serious about confessing specifically, both in terms of identifying our actions for what they are (sin) and by specifically detailing to God the particular ways we have transgressed against Him.

If I have rebelled against God through the sin of pride, I should confess my thoughts and acts of pride. If I have harbored lust in my heart, I should confess those impure thoughts. If God has instructed me to share my faith with the clerk at the hardware store, but I have neglected to do so, I should confess my disobedience to Him.

Specific confession brings about thorough cleansing and renewed power in prayer.

---

10 Author's note: I make statements concerning abortion neither lightly nor insensitively. According to statistics provided by careabortionrecovery.com, more than 1 out of 3 women will have an abortion by age 45. If this includes you, please know that there is a God who loves you, who offers forgiveness and healing to you, if you will receive it. National abortion recovery hotline: 1-866-482-LIFE

Preempt the Enemy

In Ephesians 6, Paul goes to great lengths to teach Christians how to prepare for battle, including the detailing of the "Armor of God" (vv. 10–17) that believers are to put on. Why must we do this? Paul states the purpose in verse 12: "For our struggle is not against flesh and blood, but against the rulers, against the authorities, against the powers of this dark world and against the spiritual forces of evil in the heavenly realms" (Ephesians 6:12).

There is constant warfare going on all around us in the spiritual realm, and one of the ways we prepare for it is through prayer. In verse 18 of this passage, Paul adds, "And pray in the Spirit on all occasions with all kinds of prayers and requests. With this in mind, be alert and always keep on praying for all the Lord's people." This is how Paul caps his instruction on spiritual warfare—with a command to pray.

But when we pray our "warfare" prayers, we must be fervent, diligent. Peter says, "Be alert and of sober mind. Your enemy the devil prowls around like a roaring lion looking for someone to devour" (1 Peter 5:8).

Thankfully, we need not fear our enemies because "You, dear children, are from God and have overcome them, because the one who is in you is greater than the one who is in the world" (1 John 4:4).

We also need not fear because God has given us weapons. He has given us weapons like the Armor of God, and these "weapons we fight with are not the weapons of the world. On the contrary, they have divine power to demolish strongholds. We demolish arguments and every pretension that sets itself up against the knowledge of God, and we take captive every thought to make it obedient to Christ" (2 Corinthians 10:4–5). These arguments and pretension of which Paul writes are schemes that originate with our enemy, Satan.

God has not only given us tools to defend against the devil and his minions, but also the authority to overcome them. That authority comes from five things detailed in scripture. They are: the name of Jesus (Acts 16:18), the blood of Jesus (1 John 1:7; Revelation 12:11), the Word of God (Ephesians 6:17), the word of our testimony (Revelation 12:11), and not loving our own lives, even to the point of death (Revelation 12:11).

Because this warfare is spiritual, and since our communication with God is spiritual, we find that prayer is just as much the battleground upon which the war is waged as it is a weapon or a tool to be used against Satan and the forces of darkness. Thankfully, we can prevent him gaining a stronghold in our lives as we remember this truth: "Submit yourselves, then, to God. Resist the devil, and he will flee from you. Come near to God and he will come near to you" (James 4:7–8)[11].

This enables us to preempt the work of "the thief [who] comes only to steal and kill and destroy" (John 10:10a).

11 See comments on protection in Chapter 3, *The Paradigm Of Prayer.*

Procure-Committed Partners

Prayer with other believers is an important part of life in the body of Christ (the church). According to Acts 2:42, the first century church met regularly to learn from the Apostles' teaching, to break bread, and to pray together (Acts 2:42).

We all need the benefits that come from praying with committed prayer partners. Praying with others encourages and unifies us with a unique bond found only in living the Christian life together. Matthew Henry wrote, "Praying friends are valuable friends; and it well becomes the greatest and best men to desire the prayers of others. Let us show that we value our friends, and their prayers."[12]

For someone who is struggling with the burden of a broken road, hearing another believer pray on their behalf can produce true joy and meaningful fellowship in the midst of a time of despondence. Our shared intercession can also nurture within us a greater love and spirit of concern for each other.

The idea that our prayer becomes more likely to move God's hand if larger numbers are involved is not a scriptural one, however. If it were, we would be able to "gang up" on God to see our prayers answered! This mistaken notion comes primarily from a misinterpretation of Matthew

12 Matthew Henry, *Matthew Henry's Concise Commentary On The Whole Bible* (Nashville: Thomas Nelson, Inc., 1977), 774.

18:19–20, where Jesus stated: "I tell you that if two of you on earth agree about anything you ask for, it will be done for you by my Father in heaven. For where two or three come together in my name, there am I with them."

The reason this is misunderstood is because it is frequently taken out of context. These verses come from a larger passage of scripture, which deals with the issue of church discipline of a member who is in sin. To interpret this passage as promising believers carte blanche for anything they agree to ask for, is not only grossly unscriptural, but it contradicts the sovereignty of God.

Pray with Christ's Bride at Heart

If we all need the benefit of praying together, then it stands to reason that, as we pray, we should do so with the church at heart. In his book, *When God Says No*, Thomas Hauff says, "Always keep in mind that your life is wrapped up in the body of Christ (that is, your fellow believers) and in Christ himself. Your requests should reflect what is important to both of them."[13]

Paul compared a husband-wife relationship to that of Christ and his bride, the church. He wrote: "Christ loved the church and gave Himself up for her to make her holy, cleansing her by the washing with water through the

13 Thomas R. Hauff, *When God Says No: Reshaping Prayer And Learning To Listen* (Eugene: Resource Publications/Wipf and Stock Publishers, 2011), 312.

word, and to present her to Himself as a radiant church, without stain or wrinkle or any other blemish, but holy and blameless" (Ephesians 5:25–27).

If Jesus gave so much of himself for the church, should we, His followers, be any less committed to his Bride? Part of that commitment includes the quality of our prayer on her behalf.

Pray with Maturity in Mind

As we traverse life's wilderness on our broken roads, at some point it becomes necessary to ask ourselves, "Will I be more mature spiritually if God says 'yes' to my prayer?" If we choose to be honest with ourselves, then we know that many times our prayers are just requests for God to change uncomfortable circumstances in our lives. Selfishly, we ask God to deliver us from the trial and place us squarely back inside our comfort zone, instead of asking What is it you're trying to teach me through this experience, God? or Is there a specific purpose you're preparing me for, Lord?

If we will be doubly honest, then we are forced to admit that having God magically make our problems disappear does not create the maturity and wisdom that having to struggle and rely on God will. It is to produce these fruits and more that He will, from time to time, allow a broken road experience in our lives.[14]

14 More on this in Chapter 7, *The Wilderness Of Purpose.*

Pray for Anointing

What is "anointing," and why should we pray for it? In antiquity, when a person was ceremonially anointed, it meant that they were having a divine or holy office conferred upon them. In 1 Samuel we find such an occurrence: "So Samuel took the horn of oil and anointed him [David] in the presence of his brothers, and from that day on the Spirit of the Lord came powerfully upon David" (1 Samuel 16:13).

In Psalm 23, David told God, "You anoint my head with oil" (Psalm 23:5b). The original Hebrew word for "anoint" is *dashen,* which literally means "to grow fat" or "to become prosperous." So with regard to the New Testament believer, we could describe the anointing of the Spirit as allowing Him to "grow fat" in us. It is the ability of the Holy Spirit to work through us in a mighty way.

In Ephesians 3:20, Paul told believers that God "is able to do immeasurably more than all we ask or imagine, according to his power that is at work within us." What enables the Holy Spirit to accomplish more than we "ask or imagine" through us? His anointing.

This anointing can be a puzzling thing for some Christians, primarily because of the confusing semantics involved. We hear terms like "anointed," "filled with the Spirit," "a deeper work," "the second blessing," "a second work of grace," "the fullness of the blessing," or "being baptized in the Spirit." These are all labels that, for better or worse, are tempered by denominational heritage or by generation.

The terminology of anointing is not terribly important, however. What is important is that we get it! Paul taught us that if we are in Christ, we have the gift of the indwelling of God's Holy Spirit (Romans 8:9). Being *filled* with the Spirit, then, is not simply having the Spirit abiding in us, but the transition from His abiding presence to His anointing presence in and upon our lives. In simpler terms, it is not us getting all of the Holy Spirit—which we already have—but rather the Spirit grabbing hold of all of us.

Paul said in Ephesians 5:18: "Do not get drunk on wine, which leads to debauchery. Instead, be filled with the Spirit." He knew there was no suitable substitute—chemical or otherwise—for the Holy Spirit's control of a believer. But for us to experience this "filling," there are a couple of things that must transpire.

The first key to unlocking the anointing of the Spirit is submission. It is willfully yielding control of our lives to the Spirit. There is a pattern that precedes this that can often be observed in believers' lives. At some point following salvation—months, years, decades—a crisis comes. This could be a crisis of faith, character, power (not experiencing God's power to live), or of control, specifically not relinquishing control to God. God employs these crises to eventually lead us to a new brokenness of our will and a surrender to His will, leading to a new encounter of faith, an "anointing."

Pastor Homer Lindsay—most notably remembered for thirty years of service to the First Baptist Church of Jacksonville, Florida—once recounted details of an article he had read while attending seminary in Fort Worth, Texas. The Fort Worth Star-Telegram published the gripping story of a tragic plane crash. A young student pilot was making one of his final training flights. Evidently, he froze at the controls. His instructor could be heard over the radio, yelling at him, "Turn over the controls! Turn over the controls!" The student did not. Both were killed in the crash.[15]

Tragedy can often occur when those who are in training do not turn over the controls to the wiser instructor. Likewise, if we want to live with the power of the Spirit in our lives, we must relinquish control to Him.

The second key to the anointing of the Spirit is to ask in prayer. Oh, the power and the blessing we so often deprive ourselves of by simply not asking! Jesus said, "how much more will your Father in heaven give the Holy Spirit to those who ask him!" (Luke 11:13).

---

15 Denis Lyle, *Turn Over The Controls*, Sermon Index www.sermonindex.net/modules/articles/index.php?view=article&aid=22496 (accessed May 17, 2013)

The Persistence of Prayer

Now that we have examined the nature, the necessity, the paradigm and the prerequisites of prayer, we have finally arrived at the theological crux of this entire literary exercise: the principle of persistence. That word persist means "to continue firmly in a course of action despite difficulty, opposition or failure."

The first, and most obvious, question we might ask is Why? Why be persistent in our prayer life? If we persist in prayer, are we not simply "nagging" God over and over until He gives us what we ask for? Would it not be a greater demonstration of our faith to simply take our burden to God one time, leave it in His hands, then move on? Quite the opposite.

> Persistency in your prayer life demonstrates that you have great faith in God. It does not indicate a lack of faith. Persistency in prayer develops your character. Persistency in prayer guarantees God's activity—not in the sense that He will answer it

> the way you want it answered or even that He will answer it at all—but by indicating that God is active in the situation as long as He wants you to pray it through.[1]

In his foreword to Pastor Tom Elliff's book, *A Passion for Prayer*, Dr. Stephen Olford writes, "The need for persistence is designed to effect such a change in us that we conform to the character and will of the God who eagerly waits to hear our cry."[2]

Evangelist, pastor and author, R. A. Torrey argued that persistent prayer is actually a faith-building training course.

> God does not always let us get things at our first effort. He would train us and make us strong men by compelling us to work hard for the best things. There is no more blessed training in prayer than that which comes through being compelled to ask again and again and again even through a long period of years before one obtains that which he seeks from God.[3]

---

1 Ronnie W. Floyd, *How To Pray: Developing An Intimate Relationship With God* (Nashville: Word Publishing/Thomas Nelson, Inc., 1999), Kindle e-book.

2 Tom Elliff, *A Passion For Prayer: Experiencing Deeper Intimacy With God* (Wheaton: Crossway Books/Good News Publishers, 1998), Foreword.

3 Reuben Archer Torrey, *How To Pray* (Old Tappan: Spire Books/ Fleming H. Revell, 1975), 35.

Roger Hadley was prayed for again and again and again. He was a husband, a plumber, a kids' league basketball coach, and one salty cuss! I still remember having Roger as my coach as a sixth grader. He often had a surly disposition, and it was not uncommon for his instruction to be sprinkled with the occasional expletive. To say the man had a hard edge to his personality would be an understatement.

With the benefit of hindsight, I can now look back on that time and clearly see that Roger simply was not a particularly happy person. I believe that many of his acquaintances at the time could see it, too. So the Sunday that Roger chose to answer an altar call at First Baptist Church of Guymon, Oklahoma and to make public his decision to give his life to Christ, it not only created quite a stir, but it warmed many hearts.

After the time of invitation was concluded, my dad (who pastored FBC) announced Roger's decision to trust Christ for salvation, then asked for a show of hands from all across the congregation. "How many of you have prayed for Roger Hadley?" Dozens of hands from all across the room shot up. I was awestruck at the number of people who had boldly approached God's throne in prayer on behalf of Roger Hadley. Many had persevered in praying for him for a very long time.

After finishing high school and moving away from Guymon, the memory of Roger Hadley began to fade—that is, until some years later when my wife and I happened to bump into Roger and his brother at a restaurant in Oklahoma City. Then the memory of that remarkable Sunday came flooding back. Even more remarkable was his amazing change in disposition. I found this once-abrasive man to be kind, personable, thoughtful, downright delightful. God had obviously done a transformational work in Roger's life. But it had taken years of persistent prayer on the part of those who cared for Roger in order to bring him to the point of repentance and renewal.

In the exercise of persistence, I can think of no more fitting scriptural principle than Galatians 6:9. The Apostle Paul, who was teaching Galatian believers the importance of working to please the Spirit instead of their own sinful natures, said, "Let us not be weary in well doing: for in due season we shall reap, if we faint not" (KJV). The New International Version translates it this way: "Let us not become weary in doing good, for at the proper time we will reap a harvest if we do not give up" (Gal. 6:9).

Matthew Henry once declared: "If our prayers are not answered, and the salvation we wait for is not wrought for us, it is not because God is weary of hearing prayer, but because we are weary of praying."[4]

Thank God that no one gave up praying for Roger Hadley!

---

4 Matthew Henry, *Matthew Henry's Concise Commentary On The Whole Bible* (Nashville: Thomas Nelson, Inc., 1977), 689.

Biblical Examples of Persistent Prayer

The scriptures are replete with examples of persistence in seeking God. Today, some would describe it as "praying through." Over a hundred years ago, R.A. Torrey called it prayer of "importunity." Regardless of terminology, the pattern is seen clearly in the Bible.

In Genesis 18:16–33, we find Abraham repeatedly interceding for the salvation of Sodom, and in Genesis 32:24–32, there is the account of Jacob wrestling all night with God and Jacob declaring, "I will not let You go unless You bless me" (Gen. 32:26b). Jacob received God's blessing as a result.

Gideon's wavering faith was strengthened through persistence. In Judges 6:33–40, in order to reassure Gideon that Israel was going to be delivered from her enemies under Gideon's leadership, the Lord responded to his request for proof by giving him the sign of the dewy fleece (v. 38). Gideon persisted yet again, however, saying: "'Do not be angry with me. Let me make just one more request. Allow me one more test with the fleece, but this time make the fleece dry and let the ground be covered with dew.' That night God did so. Only the fleece was dry; all the ground was covered with dew" (Judges 6:39–40).

1 Samuel tells us that Hannah, who was barren and unable to conceive with her husband, Elkanah, prayed for a child for years. Verse 10 describes how she prayed in deep anguish and tears. But the Lord heard her cries, and

the scriptures record that: "Elkanah made love to his wife Hannah, and the Lord remembered her. So in the course of time Hannah became pregnant and gave birth to a son. She named him Samuel" (1 Samuel 1:19–20).

In a psalm of Thanksgiving, David declared "Seek the LORD and his strength: seek his presence continually" (1 Chronicles 16:11, ESV).

In Nehemiah 1–2, Nehemiah prayed for four months for God's favor and blessing in order that the exiled Israelites might be able to return home. And burdened for the well-being and future of his people, Daniel fasted and prayed for 21 days (Daniel 10).

Jonah prayed continual, fervent prayers of praise and repentance to God for three days and nights from inside a great fish until God moved on his behalf and Jonah was spat onto dry land (Jonah 2:1–10).

Paul urged Roman believers: "I appeal to you, brothers, by our Lord Jesus Christ and by the love of the Spirit, to strive together with me in your prayers to God" (Romans 15:30, ESV).

In his letter to the church at Ephesus, Paul also encouraged believers there to press on in prayer: "Pray at all times…Stay alert and be persistent in your prayers for all Christians everywhere" (Ephesians 6:18, NLT).

To believers at Colossae, Paul describes his associate, Epaphras, as a prayer warrior who "is always wrestling in prayer for you, that you may stand firm in all the will of God, mature and fully assured" (Colossians 4:12).

We discover in Matthew 26, Mark 14, and Luke 22 that even Jesus travailed in persistent prayer in the Garden of Gethsemane. As He continually sought the Father's will, the scripture says, "Being in anguish, He prayed more fervently, and His sweat became like drops of blood falling to the ground" (Luke 22:44, HCSB).

Persistent, passionate prayer is the common thread in each of these passages, and it was also a character trait evident in the life of George Müller. In Spiritual Secrets of George Müller, he speaks of not being discouraged by circumstance, but persevering in prayer. He wrote, "I therefore seek to 'let patience have her perfect work,' and go on in prayer, being fully assured that the Lord will not suffer me to be confounded."[5]

George Müller knew that God's timing is not always the same as ours, but he also saw that God's timing was perfect. He said, "Help comes at the right time. We may have to wait upon the Lord, yea, even a long time; but at last He helps."[6]

Müller later goes on to admonish those who give up in prayer: "They cease to ask God, and thus they lose the blessing, which, had they persevered, they would surely have

---

5 George Müller, *Spiritual Secrets of George Müller*, compiled by Roger Steer (Wheaton: Harold Shaw Publishers/OMF Books, 1985), 52.

6 *Ibid*, 57.

obtained." [7] Then he goes on to detail a particular matter which he had brought before the Lord an estimated twenty thousand times, and for which the answer came eleven and a half years after the first request!

In *How to Pray*, R. A. Torrey defines "importunate" prayer this way: "Importunate prayer is a mighty movement of the soul toward God. It is a stirring of the deepest forces of the soul, toward the throne of heavenly grace. It is the ability to hold on, press on, and wait. Restless desire, restful patience, and strength of grasp are all embraced in it."[8]

Jesus spoke specifically of the need for persistent prayer in two parables in the Gospel of Luke, which we will take the time to examine more closely.

The Friend in Need

In Luke 11:5–13, Jesus gives the Parable of the Friend in Need. This is a continuation of Christ's teaching on prayer beginning with the "Lord's Prayer" (vv. 1–4). The key to Jesus' lesson is found in verse 8.

> Then Jesus said to them, "Suppose you have a friend, and you go to him at midnight and say, 'Friend, lend me three loaves of bread; 6 a friend of mine on a journey has come to me, and I have no food to

7 *Ibid*, 91.

8 Reuben Archer Torrey, *How To Pray* (Old Tappan: Spire Books/ Fleming H. Revell, 1975), 45.

> offer him.' 7 And suppose the one inside answers, 'Don't bother me. The door is already locked, and my children and I are in bed. I can't get up and give you anything.' 8 I tell you, even though he will not get up and give you the bread because of friendship, yet because of your shameless audacity he will surely get up and give you as much as you need.

Pastor and author Bruce Larson described the Parable of the Friend in Need in Luke 11 this way:

> "Jesus emphasizes persistence. He tells the story of the man awakened by his friend's knock. At first, he is reluctant to respond. We need to remember here that a parable teaches only one lesson. This parable teaches us to be persistent in prayer. It is not a story about the nature of God. God is not in bed with His children, asleep and reluctant to answer our prayers. Jesus is telling us to approach God boldly as we would a neighbor and to ask repeatedly without giving up. God will reward our perseverance."[9]

Simply defined, the Greek word *anaideia* in verse 8 means "persistence." However, the NIV translators have rendered it as "shameless audacity." This is apropos because God would have his children approach His throne of grace

---

9 Bruce Larson, *The Preacher's Commentary Series, Vol. 26: Luke*, Gen. Editor, Lloyd J. Ogilvie (Nashville: Thomas Nelson, Inc., 1983), 194.

in prayer (Hebrews 4:16) with such bold determination to see Him respond, that they will not be put to shame by any apparent refusal or delay on God's part. This shameless audacity embodies the words "faint not" and is an expression of tremendous faith–faith which is built up along the broken road that drives us to persistent prayer.

Ask, Seek, Knock

Completing the illustration we read about the needy friend, Jesus also made this bold, yet simple, statement: "Ask and it will be given to you; seek and you will find; knock and the door will be opened to you. For everyone who asks receives; he who seeks finds; and to him who knocks, the door will be opened" (Luke 11:9–10; Matthew 7:7–8).

What makes Jesus' words here particularly relevant to the concept of persistent prayer is the original Greek construction. M.S. Augsburger explains:

> "The threefold command to ask, seek, and knock is both command and invitation. These words are present imperatives in the Greek which mean continuous action. Ask and keep asking. This may suggest persistent effort, but more likely it is the recognition that we need to continually come to God. We should not think that, having asked once, we are presumptuous to ask again. In fact the progression suggested in the words 'ask,' 'seek,' 'knock' may suggest growing awareness of our dependence upon God."[10]

10 M.S. Augsburger, *The Preacher's Commentary Series, Vol. 24: Matthew*, Gen. Editor, Lloyd J. Ogilvie (Nashville: Thomas Nelson, Inc., 1982), 18.

In effect, Jesus is teaching us to ask and keep on asking, to seek and keep on seeking, and to knock and keep on knocking until God has responded.

According to Matthew Henry, we should:

> Pray. Pray often. Make a business of prayer, and be serious and earnest in it. Ask as a beggar asks alms. Ask as a traveller asks the way. Seek, as for a thing of value that we have lost. Knock, as he that desires to enter into the house knocks at the door.[11]

The Persistent Widow

Jesus again takes up the subject of persistent prayer in Luke 18:1–8, in the Parable of the Persistent Widow. The key statements are found in verses 1 and 7.

> Then Jesus told his disciples a parable to show
> them that they should always pray and not give up.
> 2 He said: "In a certain town there was a judge who
> neither feared God nor cared what people thought.
> 3 And there was a widow in that town who kept
> coming to him with the plea, 'Grant me justice
> against my adversary.' 4 For some time he refused.
> But finally he said to himself, 'Even though I don't
> fear God or care what people think, 5 yet because
> this widow keeps bothering me, I will see that she

11 Matthew Henry, *Matthew Henry's Concise Commentary On The Whole Bible* (Nashville: Thomas Nelson, Inc., 1977), 869.

> gets justice, so that she won't eventually come and attack me!'" 6 And the Lord said, "Listen to what the unjust judge says. 7 And will not God bring about justice for his chosen ones, who cry out to him day and night? Will he keep putting them off? 8 I tell you, he will see that they get justice, and quickly. However, when the Son of Man comes, will he find faith on the earth?"

Let's shed some cultural light on this parable for a moment—bearing in mind that the thematic current that runs through this passage is one of justice, while the context of this parable is still within Jesus' teaching on prayer. The widow in question found herself in a truly impossible situation. The judge was part of a legal system that, in Jesus' day, was often corrupt, with judges taking on only the cases where the biggest bribe was paid. To make matters worse, women in that culture were considered by most to be second-class citizens with little or no legal recourse. Her persistence was birthed by sheer desperation. If anyone could say he or she was traveling a "broken road," it was she.

As a result of her impossible predicament, she kept bothering the judge (v. 5). The Greek word here for "bother" is *parecho*. It basically means "to cause another trouble." The literal meaning of the word "attack" in verse 5 is "to give one a black eye." Her persistent "assault" finally moved the judge to give her justice.

Am I suggesting that, in order to see our prayers answered, we are somehow supposed to bully, pester or nag God until He gives us what we want? Of course not. Remember: prayer is all about seeing the will of God done, not our own. What Jesus would have us learn here is that, with the same passion and determination with which the widow pursued justice from the judge, we are to seek God's will in prayer.

Instead of instructing us to bully God—as if such a thing were actually possible—Jesus is teaching that God promises, in answer to our prayer, to vindicate His own, to right wrongs, to do justice. If an unrighteous, secular judge will eventually hear our appeals, how much more can we trust that our appeals will be heard by the only Righteous Judge, who loves us with complete abandon? And in hearing our appeals, will He not also prove Himself just and powerful?

The widow's case demonstrates how impossible situations were tailor-made for persistent prayer, because it is in the impossible that God receives the greatest glory!

Brian Lowery, editor of *Preaching Today*, discusses the fine line between being bold and bullheaded our prayers:

> I was born in the waning days of vinyl records. I would watch as my father pulled them from their sleeves and placed them on the turntable. When the needle dropped into the record's grooves, the speakers popped to life with a tide of white noise

that was chased away by music. Some records were so worn that they hiccupped along or—even worse—repeated a section, over and over again.

"The sound of a broken record—such are my prayers at times. The yellowed pages of my journals betray my stubborn consistency about this request or that concern. I rap on God's door, morning, noon, and night, half wishing I could blow the great house down and see some results!

"I often reflect on the spirited persistence of my prayers; there is a fine line between bold and bullheaded. But in my pondering, I think back on the great texts on prayer and the great prayers themselves. Alongside honesty and deep worship, you will most often find the quality of persistence. It seems the hiccupped, repetitious sounds from another room are music to the ears of God. He listens along with us. At times, he even sets the needle right.[12]

How Long Do I Persist?

God honors persistent prayer. But in all of our discussion of why to persist, we have neglected another important question: How long? How do we know just how long we are to persist? The answer is simple enough.

12 Brian Lowery, *The Beauty of a Broken Record*, PreachingToday.com http://www.preachingtoday.com/illustrations/2007/december/2122407.html (accessed May 22, 2013)

First, we can stop praying when God makes it crystal clear that the request we are placing before Him is not within His will for us. Second, and most obvious, we cease when God gloriously grants our request!

However, one other thing that is pivotal to answering the question at hand is the matter of burden—the heavy load of concern God places upon a human heart. Without burden, fervent prayer cannot even begin. The great Watchman Nee once wrote: "Burden is the secret of prayer. If a person does not feel within him burden to pray for a particular matter, he can hardly succeed in prayer."[13]

A key in knowing when the time has come to desist instead of persist is whether or not the burden placed upon our hearts is still alive. Has God removed the burden yet?

Pastor Ronnie Floyd sums it up like this:

> The burden that God gives you is a wake-up call. If God gives you the burden, it signifies He is active in the situation. Therefore, you keep praying it through until He releases you. How do you know when He releases you? He releases you when the situation is answered just the way you have prayed for it. He releases you when the situation is irreparable. He

13 Watchman Nee, *Let Us Pray* translated from Chinese (Richmond: Christian Fellowship Publishers, 1977), 39.

> releases you when He removes your burden and replaces it with peace.[14]

So is persistence in prayer appropriate for us? Is it scriptural? Yes! Not only is it so, but it is actually God's desire for us to seek Him that way. Clearly, not just in Jesus' teaching, but in the whole of scripture we find examples of persisting in our supplications to God. It is God's will for us to be consistent and diligent in our requests. He also wants us to declare our dependence upon Him. What better way can we proclaim that than by continually voicing our requests to Him?

---

14 Ronnie W. Floyd, *How To Pray: Developing An Intimate Relationship With God* (Nashville: Word Publishing/Thomas Nelson, Inc., 1999), Kindle e-book.

The Waiting of Prayer

When traveling one of life's broken roads, our minds can become unusually pre-occupied with one of two questions: Why? or When? (or some combination thereof).

In my own wilderness experiences, more often than not, the question for me has been When, Lord? When will you move on my behalf? I know that God is sovereign, that nothing in this world takes place without Him either causing it or allowing it to happen, and I know that even the things that occur that I perceive as bad can still be used to accomplish His purposes for me. Therefore, I already know the "why," at least in a general sense. As Paul put it, God is working all things "for the good of those who love him, who have been called according to his purpose" (Romans 8:28). What is that ultimate purpose? In short, to change us and bring glory to Him.[1]

This brings us to the other question, When?

---

1 This is a question that will be answered in full in Chapter 7, *The Wilderness Of Purpose.*

I believe that there is something within human nature that makes impatience universal. At some point in life, everyone seems to exhibit some degree of impatience, so it comes as no surprise when we, like the psalmist, cry out: “My soul is in deep anguish. How long, Lord, how long? Turn, Lord, and deliver me; save me because of your unfailing love” (Psalm 6:3–4), or “How long, Lord? Will you forget me forever? How long will you hide your face from me?” (Psalm 13:1).

Like both the psalmist and Job, who have uttered these two words repeatedly, this is a natural question for us. As we prayerfully traverse the path of hardship God has allowed in our lives, we cannot help but ask, Lord, when will this be over? Or why is it taking so long for you to respond to my pleas?

The waiting takes us to a place far beyond our normal comfort zone. But consider what Matthew Henry said 300 years ago regarding God’s delays:

> We are afflicted in body, state, name, and in our relations; and think all these things are against us, whereas they are really working for us a weight of glory. Thus does the Lord Jesus conceal himself and his favor, thus he rebukes and chastens those for whom he has purposes of love. By sharp corrections and humbling convictions he will break the stoutness and mar the pride of the heart, and bring to true repentance. Yet before sinners fully

> know him, or taste that he is gracious, he consults their good, and sustains their souls, to wait for him. May we do thus, never yielding to discouragement, determining to seek no other refuge, and humbling ourselves more and more under his mighty hand. In due time, he will answer our petitions, and do for us more than we can expect.[2]

The silence we sometimes experience in response to the question of How long? can be almost overwhelming. It is disheartening when it appears to us that, for whatever reason, God did not come through.

Maw and Paw were driving to town one Saturday in their banged up, rusty, 1971 Ford pickup truck. As they puttered down the road at a pace about 15 miles per hour below the speed limit, a bright red sports car came screaming down the farm-to-market road behind them. It quickly passed them and went on, but as the car passed, Maw glanced over and spotted a young couple sitting so close together that the girl was virtually sitting in the boy's lap.

Maw glanced across the cab of their old pickup, noting the amount of distance between her and Paw. She asked, "Paw, how come we don't sit like that no more?"

Paw replied, "Maw, I ain't the one who's moved!"

---

2 Matthew Henry, *Matthew Henry's Concise Commentary On The Whole Bible* (Nashville: Thomas Nelson, Inc., 1977), 63-64.

When we are in the midst of a wilderness experience, it is easy for us to believe God has left us. Somehow we convince ourselves that God has turned his back on us. Rest assured, that even on the broken road, God is with us. "God has said, 'Never will I leave you; never will I forsake you'" (Hebrews 13:4). If He seems distant, it is because we have moved away from Him.

Even Jesus' own cousin, John the Baptist, questioned the Savior in a time when he expected deliverance from his trials. In Matthew 11:2–3, the Bible says, "When John heard in prison what Christ was doing, he sent his disciples to ask him, 'Are you the one who was to come, or should we expect someone else?'" In other words, "What are you waiting for? I need you to get me out of this mess!"

Like John the Baptist, we sometimes ask the same question, not realizing that the reasons for God's delays are actually very simple.

Our Request Is Amiss

One reason God delays or denies is because we have made an inappropriate prayer request. James 4:3 says, "When you ask, you do not receive, because you ask with wrong motives, that you may spend what you get on your pleasures." The King James translation calls this asking "amiss." The word means "inappropriate."

Author Larry Crabb describes asking amiss this way:

> When I was 10, I first heard Matthew 21:22, where Jesus, who never lies, said, 'If you believe, you will receive whatever you ask for in prayer.' It was the 'whatever' model of prayer—believe, ask for whatever you want, and it's yours. I remember running outside, standing on our driveway, closing my eyes real tight, and praying: God, I want to fly like Superman. And I believe you can do it. So I'll jump, and you take it from there. I jumped four times—and each time landed half a second later and half a foot farther down the driveway. I had believed and I had asked, just like Jesus said. But I didn't receive. Thus began my 50-year journey of confusion about prayer.[3]

Asking amiss is nothing new. The three most well-known of Jesus' disciples—Peter, James and John—accompanied Jesus to the top of a high peak that Bible scholars call the "Mount of Transfiguration." It was there that suddenly God's full glory came to rest upon Jesus (see Matt. 17:1–9; Mark 9:2–9; Luke 9:28–36). The three disciples watched in awe. Their eyes beheld the glorious splendor of God just a few feet away. And they were so moved by Jesus' transfiguration that they said, "Jesus, allow us to build shelters up here, and we'll just live up here the rest of our lives, and we'll bask in your glory" (my paraphrase). Jesus did not grant their request. He did not grant it because it

3 Larry Crabb, "Great Expectations," *Pray!* magazine (Colorado Springs: NavPress, 2006), 34.

was not the right request. Their desire was not in keeping with God's desires and His plan for Jesus.

We find James and John again in Mark 10:35–37, where they went to Jesus and asked if they could make reservations for the most prestigious place in Heaven they could conceive. They said, "Let one of us sit at your right and the other at your left in your glory" (v. 37). But once again, the request was denied, because once again they had made an improper one. We can only speculate as to the true reasons for such a request, but it seems very likely that James and John were motivated by thoughts of self-glory. Wrong request and wrong motive. Thus, the answer was "no."

We find yet another example in Luke 9:51-56, where Jesus and the disciples were denied passage through a certain part of Samaria. This denial aggravated the disciples so much that they requested that Jesus consume the entire region with fire from heaven. But instead of granting their request, Jesus rebuked them.

As Jesus later stated in Luke 19:10, his purpose on earth was to "seek and save the lost." He came to transform, not to torch. The disciples' request was motivated by the craving for retribution. Jesus' denial of their request was motivated by compassion.

So we see that even Jesus' own disciples were capable of making inappropriate requests of Him. And when the requests were wrong, Jesus said "no."

We, too, are more than capable of making wrong requests of God. We probably already have and, no doubt, will again in the future. Even worse still is the fact that we are capable of making requests that are totally self-serving, overtly materialistic, convenience-minded, short-sighted, and just downright immature.

Fortunately for us, one of the most wonderful qualities of God is that, in His infinite wisdom and compassion, He loves us far too much to say yes to wrong requests.

When we are desperate to see any kind of movement of God's hand, it's easy to think that God has not answered our prayer, but the truth is that He has answered. If the request was wrong, His answer was "no."

Those of us who are parents ought to understand that "no" is not a dirty word. When God says no, we must bear in mind that not everyone who says no to us is being selfish. All manner of people—parents, a boss, even a pastor—may say no to protect us. Should we expect God to do anything less?

Hauff writes that "a 'no' is a quite useful answer in the growth process if we receive it honestly. It should be a learning experience that makes us reflect on what we asked for, and figure out how we might make better requests in the future."[4]

So when we pray earnestly about a matter, but begin to sense some resistance from the Lord, it is vital that we

---

4 Thomas R. Hauff, *When God Says No: Reshaping Prayer And Learning To Listen* (Eugene: Resource Publications/Wipf and Stock Publishers, 2011), 206.

review the request. The request might be destructive, self-serving, shortsighted, or even too small. Self-reflection is required until we are able to discern whether the request needs to be adjusted or discarded.

Our Timing Is Amiss

Sometimes we find in our prayer life that if the timing of a request is wrong, God will say, "Wait."

Because of our natural bent toward impatience, the words "not yet" or "wait" rank as some of the most despicable words in the English language, and we revert back to asking the How long? questions again. The child in each of us still wants God to meet every need, to grant every request, to move every mountain instantly.

And when our infinitely wise Heavenly Father deems it best to declare to us, "not yet," our response to Him often reveals our immaturity. But God, I want this right now! Not three months from now, not three weeks from now, not three days from now. God, read my lips: I want it now, now, now!

Of course, God is not intimidated by our childish fixation on instant gratification. We can kick and scream (figuratively or literally) all we want, but His answer is still "not yet."

It is important for us to understand, however, that God's delays are not necessarily God's denials—that often God is not saying no, He is merely saying, "Not quite yet. Trust me. I know what I'm doing. I've got my reasons."

His wisdom is trustworthy and His reasoning is beyond our comprehension. "'My thoughts are not your thoughts, neither are your ways my ways,' declares the Lord. 'As the heavens are higher than the earth, so are my ways higher than your ways and my thoughts than your thoughts'" (Isaiah 55:8–9).

The truth that "my ways are higher than your ways; my thoughts are higher than your thoughts," ought to be one reason for us—as Jesus said—to "pray and not give up" (Luke 18:1). Sometimes our requests are good and proper and right. But for reasons known only to Him, He may choose to say, "Wait. I will do this in my time."

There are some possible reasons God may have for his "wait" answers—not the least of which is that He may desire to carefully orchestrate a greater blessing than we may have had sufficient faith to pray for in the beginning. Other reasons for delay might include concerns over the need for us to develop deeper character, or the need for us to learn endurance, trust, patience, or submission—all while God is orchestrating the timing of the answer to prayer. How unfortunate it is that, when we're on the broken road, our natural tendency is to be much more concerned about our own comfort and convenience than we are about building the character that comes through patiently trusting in God's timing.

When God says "wait," we often find that the prayers with the sweetest answers are the ones that we have entrusted to Him for a long, long time.

Our Lives Are Amiss

Sometimes, there is a flaw in us personally. As a result, God denies or delays our request in order to correct the problem and to help us grow to greater spiritual maturity.

Unfortunately, the nature of our flesh is such that it is a lot easier to point the finger at God for not answering prayer than it is to look in the mirror and to say, "Maybe I am the problem." Multitudes of people have grappled with the mystery and the agony of unanswered prayer, but how many have the humility to come before a holy and just God and honestly say, "God, is it me? Am I the obstacle to the miracle that I am praying for?"

More often than not, that's not the question. It is usually, "God, why aren't you moving my mountain?" Unanswered prayer is often a reason to take a spiritual inventory and say, "Maybe it is me," and sometimes, what we find is unpleasant.

We Are Not God's Children

Chapter 1, The Nature of Prayer, established the fact that prayer is a spiritual endeavor. Romans 8:16 says "the Spirit himself testifies with our spirit that we are God's children." But until that time that our spirits come alive through faith in Christ, we are not His children and our spirits are "dead in our transgressions and sins" (Ephesians 2:1). Our direct line to God is non-functional if we are not His children.

Paul wrote to the Corinthians: "Examine yourselves as to whether you are in the faith. Test yourselves. Do you not know yourselves, that Jesus Christ is in you?—unless indeed you are disqualified" (2 Corinthians 13:5).

Some people have never connected with God in prayer because they have never come to that conscious moment of decision to truly trust Him for salvation and eternal life—even some who claim to be Christians already.

We Pray Our Own Will

Matthew Henry once wrote, "Let God's will be your rule, and his favor shall be your happiness."[5]

The necessity of praying God's will instead of our own is a concept we discussed at length in Chapter 3 and also briefly in Chapter 4. Suffice it to say, it is vital that we ensure our prayers are in line with His will.

1 John 5:14 says, "This is the confidence we have in approaching God: that if we ask anything according to his will, he hears us" (emphasis mine). The flip side of this prayer equation must also be true then, that if we do not pray according to His will, He will not hear us.

In Psalm 37:4, David penned, "Take delight in the Lord and he will give you the desires of your heart." The Hebrew word here for "give" is *nathan*. In numerous other

---

5 Matthew Henry, *Matthew Henry's Concise Commentary On The Whole Bible* (Nashville: Thomas Nelson, Inc., 1977), 704.

places in the scripture, *nathan* is translated as appoint, ascribe, establish, insert, plant or even impose. What the psalmist is telling us is that when God is preeminent in our lives, when our focus is solely on Him and His will for us, He then implants within us the desires we should have. Never has a truer statement been spoken: "Prayer has everything to do with molding the soul into the image of God."[6]

If we Christ-followers surrender to God's will, and continue to abide in Christ (John 15:4–7), then His Word abides in us and we can pray whatever we will because—strangely and wonderfully—what we desire now is what God desired first! As the late Adrian Rogers once said, "The prayer that gets to heaven is the prayer that starts in heaven."[7]

We Ignore Our Own Sin

Often, the reason for unanswered prayer is uncleanness in the human heart. Consider these scriptures:

Psalm 66:18: "If I had cherished sin in my heart, the Lord would not have listened." In other words, if I am leading a life of disobedience to God, the Lord will not hear my prayers.

---

6 Edward Mckendree Bounds, *The Necessity Of Prayer* (Memphis: Bottom Of The Hill Publishing, 2010), 46.

7 Adrian Rogers, *What Every Christian Ought To Know* (Nashville: Broadman & Holman Publishers, 2005), 218.

Isaiah 59:2 says, "your iniquities have separated you from your God; your sins have hidden his face from you, so that he will not hear."

Psalm 24:3–4 asks, "Who may ascend the hill of the LORD? Who may stand in his holy place? He who has clean hands and a pure heart." If we want to boldly approach the throne of God in prayer, we must first be certain that we are walking in holiness.

The sin that hinders our prayer life could be any number of things. It could be sins of thought or attitude. In a rebuttal to the Pharisees' claims that Jesus' disciples had defiled themselves, Jesus declared, "But the things that come out of a person's mouth come from the heart, and these defile them. For out of the heart come evil thoughts—murder, adultery, sexual immorality, theft, false testimony, slander. These are what defile a person" (Matthew 15:18–20a).

Jesus taught us that murder and adultery begin in the heart (Matthew 5:21–22, 28). In fact, all sin begins with the thoughts and attitudes we harbor within (James 1:14–15)—all the more reason to start there with our confession.

Of course, the thoughts we sometimes coddle often end up coming out of our mouths. Jesus said that "the mouth speaks what the heart is full of" (Matthew 12:34; Luke 6:45).

So the next category of sin we often need to confront includes sins of speech. To this issue Paul wrote, "Do not let any unwholesome talk come out of your mouths, but only what is helpful for building others up according to their needs, that it may benefit those who listen" (Ephesians 4:29). And Jesus warned, "I tell you, on the day of judgment people will give account for every careless word they speak" (Matthew 12:36, ESV).

What are sins of speech? Gossip, slander, hurtful words, untruth, coarse talk and profanity all fit the bill. Particularly problematic to Christians today is the temptation to mimic the world's method of talking, especially with regard to profanity. Yet this is not a new problem. Listen to what Paul wrote in the first century:

"Let there be no filthiness nor foolish talk nor crude joking, which are out of place" (Ephesians 5:4, ESV).

"But now is the time to get rid of anger, rage, malicious behavior, slander, and dirty language" (Colossians 3:8, NLT).

Paul encouraged Timothy to "set an example for the believers in speech, in conduct, in love, in faith and in purity" (1 Timothy 4:12).

In Psalm 39:1 (NASB), David wrote, "I will guard my ways that I may not sin with my tongue; I will guard my mouth as with a muzzle."

Unanswered prayer could also be due to disharmony in relationships. It would benefit us to periodically take inventory of the relationships we have with others, and ask questions like: Have I hurt or offended anyone? Treated someone dishonorably? Am I harboring bitterness toward someone who has hurt me? Am I neglecting my times of togetherness with other believers?

In Matthew 5:23–24, Jesus warned that if there is relational discord, conflict between us and others, or if there are friendships in shambles, then it disrupts our ability to have proper fellowship with God. In this passage, Jesus teaches, "If someone has been hurt by you, drop everything and attempt to reconcile that relationship. Then go back to the altar to worship and pray" (my paraphrase).

But what if someone has injured us? What should we do then? In Matthew 18:15, Jesus instructs, "if your brother sins against you, go and tell him his fault between you and him alone. If he hears you, you have gained your brother."

These principals apply equally to marital relationships. The Apostle Peter wrote: "Husbands, in the same way be considerate as you live with your wives, and treat them with respect as the weaker partner and as heirs with you of the gracious gift of life, so that nothing will hinder your prayers" (1 Peter 3:7)[8]. Of course, the reverse is true, too. Wives ought to live with their husbands in an understanding way.

The Bible's counsel in maintaining right relationships is sobering. Clearly, our priority is to make damaged relationships right. But we often fail to do so, instead harboring unforgiveness—the single most common poison that

8 Examination of the original Greek here yields a better understanding of the verse. The word translated as "vessel" or "partner" is *skeuos,* which means *a useful container or instrument.* "Weaker," from the Greek *asthenes*, means *fragile.* Peter is suggesting that husbands treat wives the same as a very delicate and useful vessel—one to be honored as precious.

affects God's people. The great irony is that it is, figuratively speaking, a poison that we administer to ourselves while expecting the other person to die!

It is impossible to love another and hold bitterness or unforgiveness against him or her at the same time. If we do, then we don't love them as Christ loved us, and if we don't keep Jesus' commandments, then it proves we do not love Him. Jesus said in John 14:24, "Anyone who does not love me will not obey my teaching."

In Matthew 18, in the parable of the unmerciful servant, Jesus taught us that God treats us with the same sort of forgiveness we offer to each other. He made this same teaching clear and plain in Matthew 6:15: "But if you do not forgive others their sins, your Father will not forgive your sins."

This unforgiveness can block God from answering our prayers. Mark 11:25 says, "when you stand praying, if you hold anything against anyone, forgive them, so that your Father in heaven may forgive you your sins."

Another area of sin to consider is dishonorable treatment of God. We find a fitting example in Malachi, a book which frequently employed a literary device called a "didactic dialectic"—in which the Lord made a charge against His people, followed by posing the very thought or question that they would raise in response, and ending with a rebuttal to that question.

In Malachi 1, in spite of unmistakable instruction from God to offer only the best lambs for worship sacrifices unto the Lord, the Israelites decided to take their best lambs to market to fetch the highest price possible. However, they would pick out the worst lambs in their flocks—lame, blind, the ones who were no good or ready to die—and they would offer those blemished lambs as worship offerings to God. God addressed this problem through the prophet: "'Go ahead, beg God to be merciful to you! But when you bring that kind of offering, why should he show you any favor at all?' asks the Lord of Heaven's Armies" (Malachi 1:9, NLT).

What God is telling them is: "After disobeying me and dishonoring me, you have the impudence to seek my blessing? You must be joking! You mock me with your disobedience, and without batting an eyelash you make your requests, fully expecting me to grant them? Why should I honor yours when you don't honor mine?"

There are a multitude of transgressions that hinder our prayers that we could discuss, but whatever the sin, all of them fall into one of two categories. There are sins of commission, things like fornication, stealing, dishonesty, destructive habits, idolatry (making anything more important than God), and so forth.

Then there are sins of omission. These would include failing to obey the Lord's commands or to conform to Christ's character, neglecting God in a personal time of prayer and the Word, neglecting regular worship, refusing to share one's faith or to employ a spiritual gift—basically, any good thing that we know we should be doing but are not. This is why James wrote: "If anyone, then, knows the good they ought to do and doesn't do it, it is sin for them" (James 4:17).

We have addressed the sin for those things that we know we have committed or omitted, but what about sins that are—for whatever reason—unknown sins? For this, we turn to King David who once wrote: "Search me, God, and know my heart; test me and know my anxious thoughts. See if there is any offensive way in me, and lead me in the way everlasting" (Psalm 139:23–24). There are times when we are so blind to our sin that we need to ask God's Holy Spirit to show us the offense in question.

When I was a junior in high school, there was a guy on our basketball team who was a real nuisance, a pest who was constantly mouthing off and running people down. One morning before first period (French class, as I recall), I decided that enough was enough. I lost my temper and we got into a scuffle. (Okay, I confess. It was not a scuffle. It was a fight!) I backed him into a corner, then punched him in the gut about eight times, and after he had breathlessly staggered away, I moved to my desk chair, thinking that I had really gotten the better of him. But later, my thumb began to throb and swell. This went on all day, and as it did, the pain increased. After school, I consulted our family doctor, Dr. Butcher (yes, that is his real name). The diagnosis: a broken thumb. Injury turned to insult when Dr. Butcher refused to treat my broken thumb until I confessed to him how I had injured it.

God's Holy Spirit is kind of like Dr. Butcher. He will put his finger on the sore spot and press hard. When He does, there will be no doubt about the sin in question. But the wondrous thing is that the Spirit convicts so that He may cleanse.

Clearly, the lack of efficacy in our prayer life can come not only from the presence of sin in our personal lives, but more specifically, the lack of confession of sin.

Matthew Henry states: "In every prayer we must make confession, not only of the sins we have been guilty of, but of our faith in God, and dependence upon him, our sorrow for sin, and our resolutions against it. It must be our confession, the language of our convictions."[9]

Our Confession and Cleansing

Incomplete confession will not work. Based on an international study of over 4,000 participants, researchers discovered that people who only partially confessed wrongdoing actually felt worse than those who chose not to confess at all. According to the study's lead author,

---

9 Matthew Henry, *Matthew Henry's Concise Commentary On The Whole Bible* (Nashville: Thomas Nelson, Inc., 1977), 782.

> Confessing to only part of the guilt of one's transgression is attractive to a lot of people because they expect the confession to be more believable and guilt-relieving than not confessing. But our findings show the exact opposite…People seeking redemption by partially admitting their big lies feel guiltier because they do not take complete responsibility for their behaviors.[10]

Confession can be a cathartic experience, when the whole truth is confessed. The word "confess" comes from the Greek word *homologeo*, which literally means to "say the same thing." It is a statement of agreement. In the context of our prayer life, it means to agree with God that we are in sin.

There is something powerful in such a confession, though, in putting the truth "out there." James, the half-brother of Jesus, knew it this. "Confess your faults one to another," he wrote (James 5:16).

King David knew it. After his adulterous affair with Bathsheba and the subsequent murder of her husband, David penned the following words:

> Have mercy on me, O God, according to your unfailing love; according to your great compassion

10 Matt Woodley, managing editor, PreachingToday.com, quoting Andrew O'Connell, *A Partial Confession Makes You Feel Worse* (Harvard Business Review/www.hbr.org), accessed February 13, 2014

> blot out my transgressions. 2 Wash away all my iniquity and cleanse me from my sin. 3 For I know my transgressions, and my sin is always before me. 4 Against you, you only, have I sinned and done what is evil in your sight…7 Cleanse me with hyssop, and I will be clean; wash me, and I will be whiter than snow. 8 Let me hear joy and gladness; let the bones you have crushed rejoice. 9 Hide your face from my sins and blot out all my iniquity. 10 Create in me a pure heart, O God, and renew a steadfast spirit within me (Psalm 51:1–4, 7–10).

David's first choice in the wake of his sins of adultery and murder was actually an attempt to conceal them. Not until the prophet Nathan confronted him about his transgressions did David "come clean."

Alexander Pope once wrote "to err is human." Well, Pope likely knew that the sin of concealment is a very human act, too! 1 John 1 contains the phrase "if we claim" three times. In this passage, John was pointing out the deceitfulness of all men. Within every human is an inborn desire to conceal the blemishes of our transgressions rather than confess them.

The problem is that one act of deceit builds upon another. The longer confession is postponed, the worse the concealment and deception gets—even to the point that we will lie to others, to ourselves, and even to God (see 1 John 1:6,8,10).

David needed a spiritual housecleaning. We need it, too. One of the marks of a true believer is that he feels dirty when he has sinned and feels the need to confess it. This confession can eliminate the obstacles that prevent God from hearing our prayer.

Our Answer of "Yes"

Pastor Tom Elliff once wrote, "Since the answer to our prayers rarely comes according to our schedule, it is important to respond properly during periods of delay. When our prayers seem to be hindered, we must continually acknowledge the sovereignty of God. Behind the delay is God's determination that we will learn how to pray."[11]

As we make the long journey of persistent prayer, agonizing through the self-examination of our motives, our expectations, even our very requests, we eventually discover that there is undeniable power in it. There will come a moment when both the request, the timing, and we, ourselves, are synchronously pure—when all the pieces of our life, character and desire beneficially intersect with God's perfect will. Then He will choose to respond with a yes.

---

11 Tom Elliff, *A Passion For Prayer: Experiencing Deeper Intimacy With God* (Wheaton: Crossway Books/Good News Publishers, 1998), 107.

Our job as we advance along the broken road of hardship, impatience and questions is to acknowledge that God is trustworthy and faithful, and that every "no" answer is bringing us one step closer to the "Yes!"

The Wilderness of Purpose

The late Corrie Ten Boom famously asked the question: "Is prayer your steering wheel or your spare tire?" Many are the times I have pondered how much less complicated life would be if God's children would break free of "spare tire syndrome." Our unfortunate tendency is to treat Him like a spiritual spare tire when things seem to be going well for us, often ignoring God. We thoughtlessly store Him away somewhere for safe keeping until crisis comes. Only when our circumstances grow beyond our ability to control them do we pull Him out of our proverbial "trunk" and begin to seek His aid for our journey down a broken road of difficulty.

While this is unfortunate, God recognizes this about us, and He uses it to His advantage, employing our affliction to drive us to our knees, fostering deeper intimacy between us and Him, and in the process, creating "lemonade" from the lemons we have made out of our lives. Whether our suffering is self-inflicted—due to the consequences of our own foolish actions—or simply something that God, in

His infinite wisdom, has chosen to allow, we ultimately find that there is purpose in it.

Long ago, Matthew Henry penned these words: "See our need of afflictions. Before, prayer came drop by drop; now they pour it out, it comes now like water from a fountain. Afflictions bring us to secret prayer."[1]

In his book, Instruments In The Redeemer's Hands, Paul David Tripp wrote: "We forget that God's primary goal is not changing our situations or relationships so that we can be happy, but changing us through our situations and relationships so that we can be holy."[2]

Holiness is God's intended result of trial. It is this wilderness purpose, and others, that we will explore together in this chapter.

We Learn to See God's Big Picture

When believers relentlessly seek God's heart in a continual process of prayer, an amazing thing happens. We begin to see life the way God sees it. Though not one to be found in Webster's dictionary, this is actually a practical definition of spiritual wisdom: the ability to adopt God's perspective on

---

1 Matthew Henry, *Matthew Henry's Concise Commentary On The Whole Bible*, (Nashville: Thomas Nelson, Inc., 1977), 657.

2 Paul David Tripp, *Instruments in the Redeemer's Hands: People In Need Of Change Helping People In Need Of Change* (Phillipsburg: P & R Publishing, 2002), 241.

all of life and its circumstances. To put things more simply, we develop a "God's-eye view," we see the "Big Picture."

A wonderful illustration of seeing the big picture is found in the work of 19th century painter, Georges Seurat. Seurat is probably best known for his painting called, Sunday Afternoon on The Island of La Grande Jatte, (which actually inspired a Broadway musical called Sunday In The Park With George).

Seurat is widely considered the father of pointillism. Pointillism is a form of painting in which tiny dots of primary colors are used to generate secondary colors. It focuses on a very specific style of brushwork used to apply the paint. Seurat's paintings are an amazing thing to behold because, from a distance, his works appear as slices of life at the circus, the park, the harbor, the opera, the beach or in the fields, usually in vibrant color. Up close, though, they appear more as a collection of teeny, tiny dots—literally thousands of infinitesimal specks of color. But from a more objective distance, the "big picture" is revealed.

The canvas of life of is made up of countless specks of details, decisions, thoughts, prayers and actions—each one capable of creating a big ripple in our proverbial "pond." All the while, the great artist, God, examines the great portrait our life is becoming. Of course, only the Lord knows what the finished product will look like, but the wondrous thing is that, as we seek His will through prayer, He begins to show us more of the big picture. These revelations help us to adjust our prayers, to begin praying His will, not our own.

Pastor Chuck Swindoll describes this wonderful by-product of prayer this way: "Prayer clears my vision. The sun 'burns through' the morning fog. Prayer does that. When you face a situation, is it foggy? Prayer will 'burn through.' Your vision will clear so you can see through God's eyes."[3]

Persistent, passionate prayer, birthed from trials, helps us to view life with a wider, eternal perspective. The Apostle Paul wrote to the church at Corinth:

> Therefore we do not lose heart. Though outwardly we are wasting away, yet inwardly we are being renewed day by day. 17 For our light and momentary troubles are achieving for us an eternal glory that far outweighs them all. 18 So we fix our eyes not on what is seen, but on what is unseen, since what is seen is temporary, but what is unseen is eternal (2 Corinthians 4:16–18).

Peter wrote:

> In all this you greatly rejoice, though now for a little while you may have had to suffer grief in all kinds of trials. These have come so that the proven genuineness of your faith—of greater worth than gold, which

---

3 Charles R. Swindoll, *Hand Me Another Brick: Timeless Lessons On Leadership* (Nashville: Thomas Nelson, Inc., 2006), 33.

> perishes even though refined by fire—may result in praise, glory and honor when Jesus Christ is revealed. (1 Peter 1:6–7)

In seeking the Father persistently, not only do we gain a better understanding of the short-term reality of our broken road, but our trials also give us a clearer picture of who God is. Job, whom God allowed to suffer tremendously with loss of wealth, family, health and more, came to realize in the end that, because of his pain, he had experienced God in a way more intimate than ever before. He said, "My ears had heard of you but now my eyes have seen you" (Job 42:5).

We Experience God's Presence

Like Job, David also understood the intimacy with God brought about by trials, and he, too, experienced God's presence in a deeper way because of them.

> For in the day of trouble, He will keep me safe in his dwelling; He will hide me in the shelter of His sacred tent and set me high upon a rock. Then my head will be exalted above the enemies who surround me; at His sacred tent I will sacrifice with shouts of joy; I will sing and make music to the Lord. (Psalm 27:5-6)

Like David, one of the benefits of fervently seeking the Lord in the midst of affliction is that we also are granted a real sense of God's divine presence in the midst of those trials. And one of the subsequent benefits of that presence is that He sends us a clear, affirming message: When we go through hard times we never have to walk alone.

Case in point: Sarai's servant Hagar. After being given as a concubine to Abram, that he might father a long-desired son, she became pregnant with Ishmael. But Hagar was soon despised by an extremely jealous Sarai and was treated unkindly. Distraught, she fled to a spring in the desert that lay beside the road to Shur. Shortly thereafter, she encountered the Angel of the Lord, who promised that if she would return He would greatly multiply her descendants, making them too numerous to count. In her flight of loneliness, she was given personal reassurance by God, so she said of Him: "You are the God who sees me…I have now seen the One who sees me" (Genesis 16:13).

Similarly, in 1 Kings 19, we find that for the prophet Elijah, great depression came in the wake of great triumph. He was on the run. Having just trumped and slain the prophets of Baal (1 Kings 18:16–40), he now had a proverbial bull's eye painted squarely on his forehead by the wicked queen Jezebel, who had vowed to take Elijah's life in retribution. The scripture says that Elijah fled "a day's journey into the wilderness. He came to a broom bush, sat down under it and prayed that he might die. 'I have had enough, Lord,' he said. 'Take my life…'" (1 Kings 19:4).

From there, God led Elijah to Mount Horeb, where He gave a supernatural demonstration of His might with a great wind that shattered the rocks of the mountains, then with an earthquake, and then a fire. Then—as if He had not gotten Elijah's attention already—God spoke to Elijah in a gentle whisper: "'What are you doing here, Elijah?' He replied, 'I have been very zealous for the Lord God Almighty. The Israelites have rejected your covenant, torn down your altars, and put your prophets to death with the sword. I am the only one left, and now they are trying to kill me too'" (1 Kings 19:13–14).

In his loneliness and dejection, God assured Elijah that not only had He appointed a successor (Elisha) to relieve Elijah in ministry, but that there were also 7,000 pure, faithful men in Israel waiting to take up God's cause.

While none of us is being pursued by an evil queen bent on our destruction, or fleeing from the chastisement of a cruel master, we do often seem to labor from the mistaken notion that if we are struggling, it is because God has abandoned us, or that somehow His plan for us has failed. Quite the contrary. Be assured that God sees us in our suffering. His presence there along the broken road reminds us that not only are we not alone, but that He is truly active in our lives.

While things might seem horribly wrong to us, struggle is frequently a sign that things are going right. "Suffering does not mean that God's plan has failed. It is the plan. Suffering is a sign that we are in the family of Christ…We suffer so that we may know him more deeply and appreciate his grace more fully,"[4] writes Paul David Tripp.

We Garner God's Strength

Along the broken road, it is not uncommon to find ourselves crying out that we simply cannot go on. The climb is too steep. The path is too rocky. Our strength is giving out. We falter. We stumble. We fall. In our brokenness, we cry "God, I need you!"

This is the exact moment when God is able to do a mighty work in our lives. This is a great truth of the Christian life, that many times God will allow, even create, circumstances in our lives that foster a greater relationship of dependence on Him. When, in our struggles, we finally come to the breaking point, realizing that we do not have the wisdom or strength to overcome our situation, and we choose to make our declaration of dependence on Him, then He proves Himself to be powerful. We have given God an opportunity to "show up and show off" in our lives. The greater our weakness, the greater His power.

The Apostle Paul, having persisted in prayer to God three times, beseeching Him to remove the metaphori-

---

4 Paul David Tripp, *Instruments in the Redeemer's Hands: People In Need Of Change Helping People In Need Of Change* (Phillipsburg: P & R Publishing, 2002), 153.

cal "thorn"[5] in his flesh, recounts God's answer to him in 2 Corinthians:

> But He said to me, "My grace is sufficient for you, for my power is made perfect in weakness." Therefore I will boast all the more gladly about my weaknesses, so that Christ's power may rest on me. That is why, for Christ's sake, I delight in weaknesses, in insults, in hardships, in persecutions, in difficulties. For when I am weak, then I am strong (2 Corinthians 12:9–10).

Paul understood that a key to successful passage on the broken road is allowing God to be our strength. Thankfully God knows our every weakness and our every need, and He graciously works on our behalf to help us make it through the trials of life. There is no situation too taxing, no moment when He forgets about us, and no obstacle too great that His strength cannot help us through.

One of the specific ways that God grants us strength in hard times is also to send us someone to share our burdens, a friend to walk the broken road with us, to shine the light of encouragement on our dark path.

Pastor and author James MacDonald writes:

---

5 The exact nature of Paul's "thorn" is unknown. Some theories include temptation, failing eyesight, malaria, migraines, epilepsy, speech disability, or demonic oppression.

> When we let others in our struggles, God blesses our humility and dispels the darkness through the comforting assurance of friendship. Often God sends along a brother or sister who really knows and has gone through something similar. More than prayer for your strength, they bring an understanding of what's ahead. They stick closer than a sibling. The way of escape may be someone who has walked this road before.[6]

Whether God chooses to empower us through the strength of the Holy Spirit, or whether He bolsters us through the strength of a friend, there is one truth we cannot deny: adversity will continually be with us. Twenty-four hours a day, seven days a week? Of course not. But struggle is a common part of the Christian life. "In fact, everyone who wants to live a godly life in Christ Jesus will be persecuted" (2 Timothy 3:12).

Thankfully, Christ has defeated the power of our trials. There is nothing that happens in this life that He, in His strength, has not already overcome. He declared in John 16:33: "I have told you these things, so that in me you may have peace. In this world you will have trouble. But take heart! I have overcome the world."

Paul addresses this triumph in Romans 8:31–39, reminding us that, because we are in Christ, and because

6 James MacDonald, *Always True: God's 5 Promises When Life Is Hard* (Chicago: Moody Publishers, 2011), 121-122.

nothing will separate us from Christ's love: "In all these things [tribulation, distress, persecution, famine, danger] we are more than conquerors through Him who loved us" (Romans 8:37).

We Learn from God's Discipline

As a parent, I cannot recall a single time when I disciplined my children that it was—in any way, shape or form—pleasant. Quite the opposite, in fact. But in order to see Ryan, Ben, Katie and Luke realize their full potential in Christ, there have been times when their mother and I have been forced to inject discipline into their personal affairs in order to teach them to make wiser choices. We do so willingly, though, knowing that the lessons learned help the kids to adopt Christlikeness.

The author of the book of Hebrews, quoting from Proverbs 3, gave this instruction:

> My son, do not make light of the Lord's discipline, and do not lose heart when he rebukes you, because the Lord disciplines the one he loves, and he chastens everyone he accepts as his son.' Endure hardship as discipline; God is treating you as his children. For what children are not disciplined by their father? (Hebrews 12:5–7).

For us, sometimes our trip down a broken road is the result of our own rebellion and foolishness, and it is God's hand of discipline that has allowed us to stumble into adversity. As a result, the persistent prayer we ought to be praying in this situation is one of humility, contrition and repentance.

However, rather than learning to recognize our broken road for what it is—an opportunity to experience God in a more intimate way—we tend to complicate our journey down the wilderness path through grumbling, complaints and ingratitude for what God is working to accomplish in our lives. Pastor and author Jeff Manion refers to the broken road as "The Land Between." As a point of illustration, he details the attitude of the children of Israel as they made their exit from Egypt.

> The Land Between is painful terrain to traverse. Often we make it more painful than it needs to be. Our actions, reactions, and overreactions can compound the situation. The journey through the desert was difficult for the Israelites, but they increased their own pain. They locked into a pattern of complaining and demanding, a pattern of ingratitude and distrust. [7]

Unlike the Israelites, we would do well to express gratitude for God's guiding hand of discipline, knowing that if God "chastens" us, He is doing so to better us, just

---

7 Jeff Manion, *The Land Between: Finding God In Difficult Transitions* (Grand Rapids: Zondervan Publishing, 2010), 127.

as any parent who truly cares for his children's well-being would do. It is an expression of merciful love. As Oswald Chambers, the early 20th century Scottish evangelist and teacher, puts it:

> We say sorrow, disaster, calamity. God says chastening and it sounds sweet to him though it is a discord to our ears. Don't faint when you are rebuked, and don't despise the chastening of the Lord.[8]

Fortunately for us, as God uses our circumstances to reveal our transgressions, and as we repentantly seek His heart in prayer, one of the blessings we discover along the broken road is that God is tremendously gracious in granting us the ability to learn from our missteps.

We Discover God's Trustworthiness

Another blessing that we discover along the broken road of persistent prayer is that God is actively at work in our lives and hearts to foster a newer, deeper sense of trust, one that is truly transformational. After all, is this not what our relationship with Him is built upon? According to Tripp: "The Christian life can really be boiled down to two words: trust and obey. I must always entrust the things that are out

8 Oswald Chambers, quoted at InspirationalStories.com www.inspirationalstories.com/quotes/oswald-chambers (accessed Jan. 17, 2015).

of my control to God, and I must always be faithful to obey his clear and specific commands."[9]

One cannot remain viable without the other. Their relationship is circular. Without consciously choosing to trust God within, we seldom take a step of obedience without. Yet it is the obedience we exercise along the broken road that leads us to experience God's trustworthiness in exciting new ways. Manion describes it this way:

> In the wilderness travels of the Israelites, God was out to grow a specific fruit in this harsh environment: He wanted to produce a relationship of trust. He desired an intimate relationship with His people, and trust is the glue that holds any relationship together. This trusting relationship with God would be critical to the people's ability to fulfill their destiny. [10]

Another one of the key elements in this equation of trust, however, is prayer. It is the sweet and frequent communion we share with God that often leads us to take the first step of expressed faith. In his book, Hand Me Another Brick, Chuck Swindoll declared: "Prayer activates

---

9 Paul David Tripp, *Instruments in the Redeemer's Hands: People In Need Of Change Helping People In Need Of Change* (Phillipsburg: P & R Publishing, 2002), 255.

10 Jeff Manion, *The Land Between: Finding God In Difficult Transitions* (Grand Rapids: Zondervan Publishing, 2010), 161-162.

my faith. After praying I am more prone to trust God. And how petty and negative and critical I am when I don't pray! Prayer sets faith on fire."[11]

Sadly, though God's desire in allowing the broken road is to foster a transformation that ensures our lives will never be the same, some never learn to embrace what God is doing. The broken road becomes the place where their faith goes to wither away and ultimately die. Remember the Israelites' downfall? What should have been a relatively brief journey for them turned into a forty year struggle. Their broken road on the way to promise was a circuitous one because they simply were not willing to embrace the transformation that comes from trusting God's heart and obeying His instruction.

When we enter into the wilderness, we would do well to heed Henry's words: "God's way is the right way, though it seems [round]about. If we think He leads not His people the nearest way, yet we may be sure He leads them the best way, and so it will appear when we come to our journey's end."[12]

God's roadmap is one intended to transform us. We should be cautioned, though. This type of transformational growth that God is working to foster within us is hardly

---

11 Charles R. Swindoll, *Hand Me Another Brick: Timeless Lessons On Leadership* (Nashville: Thomas Nelson, Inc., 2006), 34.

12 Matthew Henry, *Matthew Henry's Concise Commentary On The Whole Bible* (Nashville: Thomas Nelson, Inc., 1977), 92.

automatic. Depending on how we choose to respond, we might just as easily emerge from our broken road full of bitterness and resentment. God created us as agents of free will. We have the option of either letting the wilderness transform us or embitter us.

In our confusion and our brokenness, we still have a choice. We can turn our hearts away from God, or we can choose to trust Him.

We Understand God's Goodness

For many of us, it is upon the broken road that we fully come to realize the height, breadth, and depth of God's unfathomable goodness toward us. The ultimate promise of His goodness is found in Romans 8:28, which says: "And we know that in all things God works for the good of those who love Him, who have been called according to His purpose."

Who are those "who love Him," those "who have been called according to His purpose?" That is us—believers, Christ-followers, the children of God. Paul is telling us that God is working on the behalf of Christians in all things. But what does the Bible mean when it says "all?" Simple. It means all! Paul is not stating that God is at work in a couple of things, a number of things, or even a majority of things. God is working for our good in all things. As we persistently and passionately seek Him in the midst of the bleakest situations, we begin to see more and more just how God is using our dire straits for good.

But if God really is on our side, if He really is orchestrating every awful, despicable thing for our supposed good, what is the ultimate goal of His work? What is His end game?

Clearly, when we find ourselves in the broken seasons of life, there are two goals God is working to accomplish as we desperately seek Him out in prayer. One is change. Our wilderness struggles force us to grapple with a life-changing query: Lord, what is it within me that you are changing in this difficult circumstance?

Can we be brutally honest for a moment? This is a most painful question to ask, particularly if we are overcome with grief over the loss of a loved one, inundated with debt and the looming specter of bankruptcy, grappling with the fear that cancer brings, or battling the depression that inevitably follows the bitter end of a relationship. As we drag our bloody feet along the broken road, it is all too easy to become fixated on the thought of getting off. We do not immediately realize that the path we loathe should be a path we love. How can this be so? Because the broken road can bear the fruit in our lives that God desires most.

Due to our chronic "spare tire syndrome," more often that not, it is through these maddening seasons of calamity that God chooses to do His best work in us. Knowing this, it should come as no surprise to us then, that there can be purpose in our pain—that is, if we choose to respond to God's orchestration of our trials with open hearts and minds. His desire is to create something wondrous, beautiful and lasting within us if we will choose to cooperate with Him as He walks us down the broken road.

If God's goal is change, then what is it? What is that change? The change that God is working to accomplish in us can be found in the following verse: "For those God foreknew he also predestined to be conformed to the image of his Son, that He might be the firstborn among many brothers and sisters" (Romans 8:29, emphasis mine).

As we have discussed, the change may come in the form of learning to adopt God's point of view, in experiencing His presence or His strength more deeply, in learning from His discipline, or in realizing His trustworthiness. No matter what shape the change may take, however, God's ultimate goal for us is to be "conformed to the image of His Son," Jesus Christ. The "good" that God the Father is working in all things is to make us more like God the Son!

Not coincidentally, the place where our probing questions most often intersect His infinite good is within our prayer. It is in the outpouring of our hearts to Him, and in the sweet, divine harmony that follows, that we begin to understand why He works the way that He does, and why we must change.

Philip Yancey expounds:

> If prayer stands as the place where God and human beings meet, then I must learn about prayer. Most of

> my struggles in the Christian life circle around the same two themes: why God doesn't act the way we want God to, and why I don't act the way God wants me to. Prayer is the precise point where those themes converge.[13]

As Yancey suggests, if we will learn about prayer, if we will train ourselves to fervently and persistently seek God's heart, a remarkable thing will happen. We will discover the wonderful truth that we have come to receive a vital, active faith that shines most brightly when life seems darkest, that the most beautiful intimacy we can experience with God will have been nurtured in the rocky soil that only our trials can produce. Yes, struggle can produce beauty. So faint not. A test will one day become a testimony, and a mess will soon become God's message!

A man once found the cocoon of an emperor moth and took it home to watch it emerge. One day a small opening appeared, and for several hours the moth struggled, but could not seem to force its body past a certain point. So thinking that something must have been wrong, the man took some scissors and snipped the remaining bit of the cocoon. The moth emerged, its body large and swollen, its wings small and shriveled. The man thought that in a few hours that beautiful wings would emerge. But instead of

---

13 Philip Yancey, *Prayer: Does It Make Any Difference?* (Grand Rapids: Zondervan Publishing, 2006), Kindle e-book.

developing into a graceful butterfly, free to take flight, the moth was doomed to remain large and swollen with useless, shriveled wings for the rest of its existence.

The man did not realize that the constricting cocoon and the struggle necessary to pass through the tiny opening are God's way of forcing fluid from the moth's body to its wings, thereby facilitating a grand transformation.[14]

For us, sometimes the struggle of the broken road, and the forced necessity to seek God in prayer, is exactly what we need for God to transform us into someone beautiful, someone who is conformed to the will of God, and in so doing, one who bears the likeness of Jesus Christ.

The penultimate goal of God's orchestrations along the broken road is the change that makes us more like Jesus. Kierkegaard once said, "Prayer does not change God, but it changes the one who offers it."[15] The final goal, however, is glory, specifically God's. After all, receiving glory is His job, and it is the ultimate purpose for which we were created.

Jonathan Edwards, who was arguably the greatest preacher and theologian known in eighteenth-century America—perhaps in all of American history—wrote in his book *The End For Which God Created The World*:

---

14 Craig Brian Larson, *Illustrations For Preaching And Teaching* (Grand Rapids: Christianity Today/Baker House, 1993), 266.

15 Søren Kierkegaard, *Purity Of Heart*, rev. ed., trans. Douglas V. Steere (New York: Harper, 1948), 51.

> [God] had to respect himself, as His last and highest end, in this work; because He is worthy in Himself to be so, being infinitely the greatest and best of beings. All things else, with regard to worthiness, importance, and excellence, are perfectly as nothing in comparison of Him...All that is ever spoken of in the Scripture as an ultimate end of God's works is included in that one phrase, 'the glory of God.'[16]

We seek God in prayer that we might be changed. That is the greatest fruit of our passionate, persistent pursuit of Him along the broken road. But the greatest fruit of our subsequent change is the glory He receives from a transformed life!

> Our Father in heaven, Your name be honored as holy...For Yours is the kingdom and the power and the glory forever. Amen (Matt. 6:9, 13b, HCSB).

16 Jonathan Edwards, *The End For Which God Created The World*, in John Piper, *God's Passion For His Glory: Living The Vision Of Jonathan Edwards* (Wheaton: Crossway Books, 1998), 140, 242.

The Wealth of Prayer

We have come to the end of our journey together. We have discussed in detail what prayer is, why it is necessary, what form it should take, the precursors involved, the need for persistence, the reasons God delays, and the purpose in our struggles.

The only remaining question to ask ourselves is, "What should my prayer life look like now?"

In answer to that question, allow me to offer a brief examination of the fruits that a committed prayer life offers us.

An Earnest Way to Walk with God

In John 17, Jesus prayed for all of mankind, saying to the Father: "Now this is eternal life: that they know you, the only true God, and Jesus Christ, whom you have sent" (John 17:3, emphasis mine).

Quoting Deuteronomy 6:5, Jesus said, "Love the Lord your God with all your heart and with all your soul and with all your mind" (Deut. 6:5; Matt. 22:37).

To truly know Him and to be known, to love Him and be loved are the most wondrous privileges a Christian could hope to enjoy. It is an overwhelming blessing to think that the God of the universe desires fellowship with us. Yet the sort of deep, intimate fellowship God desires to have with us is impossible without an earnest commitment on our part to consistently seek Him in prayer. Remember how we defined prayer in chapter one? It is having a heart-to-heart talk with God.

Little Patty and Suzie vowed to be "BFFs" (best friends forever). But Suzie's dad got a transfer, and their family was forced to relocate to another state.

Patty promised, "I'll write everyday. I'll call once a week. BFFs!"

But as time passed, communication became more and more infrequent, until not only were they not best friends, but they did not know each other at all. Years later, Patty received Suzie's graduation announcement in the mail.

"Suzie? Suzie who?" she wondered.

How can we expect to really know someone we do not talk to?

Prayer is our primary means of spending time with our Heavenly Father, and if we will devote ourselves wholeheartedly to it (and Him), He will deepen the personal fellowship we enjoy with Him.

An Extensive Form of Growth in God

There are numerous vehicles of discipleship known to Christ-followers today. There is, of course, the favorite TV preacher or radio evangelist. There is the teaching received from the Sunday morning pulpit or the weeknight small group gathering. There are the insights gleaned from the writings of a favorite Christian author. There is the wise counsel offered through a Paul-Timothy partnership with an experienced mentor.

While each of these has potential merit, none of them will have life-impacting, transformational value if they are not coupled with the fervent prayer and Scripture meditation that comes during the solitary time we spend daily with God. The aforementioned methods of discipleship are mere morsels, only appetizers in a seven-course meal that is seasoned by time spent alone with God on a daily basis.

If we will devote ourselves to it, our commitment to persistent prayer will allow God to nurture discovery, wisdom, maturity, holiness, purity, and character within us, in ways far too great for us to enumerate.

An Exceptional Sensitivity to the Voice of God

To the exiles in Babylon, who were suffering the consequences of their foolish rebellion against God, Jeremiah had written these words of promise from the Lord: "'You will seek me and find me when you seek me with all your heart. I will be found by you,' declares the Lord" (Jeremiah 29:13–14a).

God wants to be found by us. Moreover, He wants His will to be known by us. It is not some great mystery He intends for us to spend our entire lives trying to uncover. And while He employs a number of different methods for divulging His will, sometimes God chooses to speak to us through the voice of the Holy Spirit. In John 10, Jesus said, "My sheep listen to my voice; I know them, and they follow me" (John 10:27).

If we truly desire to hear God's voice though, we must be fully committed to actually listening! Dag Hammersjkold once wrote, "How can you expect to keep your powers of hearing when you never want to listen? That God should have time for you, you seem to take as much for granted as that you cannot have time for Him."[1]

In his book *Becoming a Healthy Church*, Stephen Macchia articulates the need to listen for God's voice:

> We must tune our ears to hear God's voice. It's like the child who was told by his father during a symphony orchestra concert, "Listen for the flutes in this song. Don't they sound beautiful?" The child, unable to distinguish the flutes, looks up at his father with a puzzled look, "What flutes, father?" The child first needs to learn what flutes sound like

1 Dag Hammersjkold, "Markings" (Carol Stream: Christianity Today), Vol. 36, no. 11.

> on their own, separate from the whole orchestra, before he is able to hear them in a symphony. So it is with us as children of God. Unless we take the time to hear his voice in the quiet moments of life, we will not be able to hear him in the symphony sounds of life.[2]

Be assured, that as the scripture says, if we are seriously, consistently seeking God, we will find Him. But if our resolve is lackluster, then God's voice is much more difficult to distinguish from the competing cacophony of voices the world would have us listen to. As Frizzell describes it, without an adequate prayer life, we become "spiritually hard of hearing."[3]

An Expanded Supply of the Power of God

Just before His ascension into heaven, Jesus promised His disciples that, after the Holy Spirit had come upon them, they would receive power (Acts 1:8).

That same power Jesus promised them is now at work within us. But prayer is key in receiving that power. The Father gives the Holy Spirit to those who ask Him in prayer (Luke 11:13).

---

2 Stephen Macchia, *Becoming a Healthy Church* (Grand Rapids: Baker Books, 1999), 63.

3 Gregory R. Frizzell, *How To Develop A Powerful Prayer Life* (Memphis: Master Design Ministries, 1999), 4.

Power does not come, however, if we ask in a piecemeal fashion. If only God's people were as committed to consistent prayer as we are to favorite TV programs, keeping up with fashion trends, griping about the political landscape, or wasting time on Facebook, we could do powerful things for the Kingdom! In John 14:12–13, Jesus told his disciples: "Very truly I tell you, whoever believes in me will do the works I have been doing, and they will do even greater things than these, because I am going to the Father. And I will do whatever you ask in my name, so that the Father may be glorified in the Son."

Where there is little prayer, there is little power, but where there is much prayer, there is an abundance of power!

An Extraordinary Increase in Answers from God

My list of the fruits of persistent prayer is hardly an exhaustive one. As we grow and mature in our pursuit of God's heart, many other blessings will become readily apparent too.

There is, however, one last fruit to discuss. The most obvious benefit that comes from having a consistent, passionate prayer relationship with God is that we begin to see an extraordinary increase in *yes* answers from Him.

Jesus taught us that "If you abide in Me, and My words abide in you, you will ask what you desire, and it shall be done for you" (John 15:7, NKJV). Abide comes from the Greek word *meno*, which can be translated as *to be held continually*.

If we continually abide inwith Him, if we choose to take up residence in His presence, then understanding His will and letting Him place the right desires within us becomes a much simpler matter, doesn't it? As we go through long journeys of prayer with Him, we begin to understand exactly what we should have been asking for in the first place. It is always easy to get a yes when we choose to ask what God directs us to ask!

A dedicated prayer warrior will begin to see his or her prayers take on a greater power than ever before. There will be greater power to withstand the attacks of the enemy, more lost souls will come to know Jesus Christ, the needs of more loved ones will be met, and the body of believers in our local church will begin to experience awakening and revival. God will be glorified more profoundly than ever before, if—as the Lord says—"My people, who are called by My name, will humble themselves and pray and seek My face and turn from their wicked ways, then I will hear from heaven, and I will forgive their sin and will heal their land" (2 Chronicles 7:14).

Are you ready to partake of the fruits of persistent prayer? Are you ready to receive the victory that God can bring along the broken path of adversity? If you truly harbor a hunger for a greater work of the Lord in your life, for a deeper intimacy with Him, for a vibrant ministry to others, for transformation in the lives of the lost, then by all means, let us pray!

Bibliography

Augsburger, M.S. *The Preacher's Commentary Series*, Vol. 24: Matthew, Gen. Editor, Lloyd J. Ogilvie (Nashville: Thomas Nelson, Inc., 1982)

Baker's Evangelical Dictionary of Biblical Theology, Prayer, Millennium3 Online Digital Library

Bennett, Arthur ed., *The Valley of Vision: A Collection of Puritan Prayers & Devotions* (Carlisle: Banner Of Truth Trust, 1975)

Bounds, Edward Mckendree. *The Necessity of Prayer* (Memphis: Bottom Of The Hill Publishing, 2010)

Boyd, Bobby/Hanna, Jeffrey/Hummon, Marcus. "Bless the Broken Road" (Los Angeles: Bug Music, 1994)

Butler, Trent C. ed., *Holman Illustrated Bible Dictionary* (Nashville: Holman Bible Publishers, 2003)

Chambers, Oswald. quoted at Inspirational Stories, www.inspirationalstories.com

Crabb, Larry. "Great Expectations," Pray! magazine (Colorado Springs: NavPress, 2006)

Easton's Bible Dictionary, Prayer, Millennium3 Online Digital Library

Edwards, Jonathan. *The End for which God Created the World*, quoted in John Piper, *God's Passion for His Glory: Living the Vision of Jonathan Edwards* (Wheaton: Crossway Books, 1998)

Elliff, Tom. *A Passion for Prayer: Experiencing Deeper Intimacy with God* (Wheaton: Crossway Books/Good News Publishers, 1998)

Floyd, Ronnie W. *How to Pray: Developing an Intimate Relationship with God* (Nashville: Word Publishing/Thomas Nelson, Inc., 1999)

Frizzell, Gregory R. *How to Develop a Powerful Prayer Life* (Memphis: Master Design Ministries, 1999)

Hammersjkold, Dag. "Markings" (Carol Stream: Christianity Today) Vol. 36, no. 11.

Hauff, Thomas R. *When God Says No: Reshaping Prayer and Learning to Listen* (Eugene: Resource Publications/Wipf and Stock Publishers, 2011)

Henry, Matthew. *Matthew Henry's Concise Commentary on the Whole Bible* (Nashville: Thomas Nelson, Inc., 1977)

Jones, E. Stanley. *A Song of Ascents: A Spiritual Autobiography*, quoted in Charles R. Swindoll, *Swindoll's Ultimate*

Book Of Illustrations and Quotes (Nashville: Thomas Nelson, Inc., 1998)

Kierkegaard, Søren, *Purity of Heart*. New York, NY: Harper, 1948.

Larson, Bruce, *The Preacher's Commentary*. Vol. 26: Luke. Nashville, TN: Thomas Nelson, 1983.

Larson, Craig Brian. *Illustrations for Preaching and Teaching: From Leadership Journal*. Grand Rapids, MI: Baker House, 1993.

Lowery, Brian. "The Beauty of a Broken Record." Preaching Today. Accessed March 5, 2015. http://www.preachingtoday.com/illustrations/2007/december/2122407.html.

Lyle, Denis. "Turn Over The Controls." Sermon Index. Accessed May 17, 2013.

Macchia, Stephen A. *Becoming a Healthy Church: 10 Characteristics*. Grand Rapids, MI: Baker Books, 1999.

MacDonald, James. *Always True: God's 5 Promises When Life Is Hard*. Chicago: Moody Publishers, 2011.

Manion, Jeff. *The Land bBetween: Finding God in Difficult Transitions*. Grand Rapids, MI: Zondervan, 2010.

Müller, George. *Spiritual Secrets of George Müller*, compiled by Roger Steer (Wheaton: Harold Shaw Publishers/ OMF Books, 1985)

Nee, Watchman. *Let Us Pray Translated from Chinese*. Richmond: Christian Fellowship Publishers, 1977.

Nouwen, Henri J.M. *The Way of the Heart: Connecting With God through Prayer, Wisdom and Silence*. New York: Random House Publishing, 1983.

Oatman Jr., Johnson/Excell, Edwin O. "Count Your Blessings," Baptist Hymnal (Nashville: Lifeway Worship, 2008)

O'Connell, Andrew. "A Partial Confession Makes You Feel Worse." Harvard Business Review/www.hbr.org.

Olford, Stephen. *The Dynamics of Anointed Expository Preaching: Question And Answer #2*. Memphis: Olford Ministries International.

Rogers, Adrian. *What Every Christian Ought To Know: Essential Truths for Growing Your Faith*. Nashville, Tenn.: Broadman & Holman Publishers, 2005)

Swindoll, Charles R. *Hand Me Another Brick: Timeless Lessons On Leadership*. Nashville: Thomas Nelson, 2006.

Torrey, R. A. *How to Pray*. Complete and Unabridged. ed. Old Tappan, NJ: Revell, 1970.

Trench, Richard Chenevix. quoted in *The Kneeling Christian*. Grand Rapids: Zondervan Publishing, 1945.

Tripp, Paul David. *Instruments in the Redeemer's Hands: People In Need Of Change Helping People In Need Of Change*. Phillipsburg, NJ: P & R Pub., 2002.

Warren, Richard. *The Purpose-Driven Life: What on Earth am I Here For?* Grand Rapids: MI: Zondervan Publishing, 2002.

Yancey, Philip. *Prayer: Does It Make Any Difference?* Grand Rapids, MI: Zondervan, 2006.

About the Author

Eric Chaffin is an Associate Pastor at Southcrest Baptist Church in Lubbock, Texas. Since 1992, he has been involved in leading para-church ministries, in pastoral ministry and in motivational speaking. He has addressed children, teens, singles, college students, men's groups, churches, civic clubs, and other groups, numbering from 6 to 6000. Whether drug prevention lectures, abstinence education, preaching, crusades, chapel services or men's bible studies, Eric's messages have always been relevant, dynamic, and scripturally sound.

Eric's love of sports is often evident in his preaching and teaching, and he recognizes the effectiveness of expressing Biblical themes in athletic terms. He is the author of *Everything I Know About God I Learned From Football* and its sequel, *Go Deep: Gridiron Reflections On God's Playbook.* A sought-after chapel speaker, Chaffin also served as a team pastor for the Oklahoma City Yard Dawgz and the Lubbock Renegades arena football teams and has been invited to speak to such college football programs as the Texas Tech Red Raiders, the University of Kansas Jayhawks and the New Mexico Lobos.

Prior to his call to ministry, Eric spent a number of years working in radio, utilizing his talents in programming, production and as an on-air personality. His most memorable radio moments came as one half of the morning team of "Smith & Wesson" on KOLT 106 in Albuquerque, New Mexico. While in Albuquerque, Eric won local and regional "Addie" awards for best commercial spot. He also performed in five musical productions with the Albuquerque Civic Light Opera, garnering lead roles in three.

Eric holds a Bachelor's degree in Communication & Theatre from Southwest Baptist University, as well as Master of Ministry, Doctor of Ministry and Doctor of Biblical Studies degrees from Master's International School of Divinity.

Eric and his wife, Kristi, are blessed to be the parents of four children: Ryan, Ben, Katie and Luke.